*The Humanities
in American Life*

REPORT OF
THE COMMISSION
ON THE HUMANITIES

The Humanities in American Life

UNIVERSITY OF
CALIFORNIA PRESS
Berkeley / Los Angeles / London

University of California Press
Berkeley and Los Angeles, California

University of California Press, Ltd.
London, England

© 1980 by
The Regents of the University of California

Library of Congress Cataloging in Publication Data

Commission on the Humanities (Founded 1978)
  The humanities in American life.
  Includes index.
    1. Humanities. 2. United States—Intellectual
life. I. Title.
AZ103.C54 1980   001.3   80–14084
ISBN 0–520–04183–6
ISBN 0–520–04208–5 (pbk.)

Printed in the United States of America

1 2 3 4 5 6 7 8 9

CONTENTS 🌿

COMMISSION ON
THE HUMANITIES 🌿

RICHARD D. LAMM, Governor of Colorado

SHERMAN E. LEE, Director, Cleveland Museum of Art

ROBERT M. LUMIANSKY, President, American Council of Learned Societies

MARTIN E. MARTY, Professor of the History of Modern Christianity, University of Chicago

ROCH L. MIRABEAU, Dean of Arts and Sciences, Miami-Dade Community College—North Campus

THE HON. CHARLES A. MOSHER, former member of Congress (Ohio)

CHARLES MUSCATINE, Professor of English, University of California, Berkeley

WALTER J. ONG, S.J., Professor of English and Professor of Humanities in Psychiatry, Saint Louis University

HAROLD RAYNOLDS, JR., Commissioner of Education, State of Maine

HENRY ROSOVSKY, Dean of the Faculty of Arts and Sciences, Harvard University

JOHN E. SAWYER, President, Andrew W. Mellon Foundation

LEWIS THOMAS, M.D., President, Memorial Sloan-Kettering Cancer Center

DARWIN T. TURNER, Professor of English and Chairman, Afro-American Studies, University of Iowa

HELEN VENDLER, Professor of English, Boston University

HARRY WOOLF, Director, Institute for Advanced Study

Liaison with the Rockefeller Foundation

JOEL COLTON, Director for Humanities, Rockefeller Foundation

Commission Staff

GAINES POST, JR., Executive Director, Associate Professor of History, University of Texas at Austin

STEVEN YOUNG, Assistant Director

ELLEN R. WOODS, Research Associate

VIRGINIA S. NEWTON, Research Consultant

DONNA M. PINTO, Secretary

Special Advisers

JOHN I. GOODLAD, Dean, Graduate School of Education, University of California, Los Angeles

LEROY LOVELACE, Chairman, English Department, Wendell Phillips High School, Chicago

RICHARD MACKSEY, Director, Center for the Humanities, Johns Hopkins
   University
PHILLIP WOODRUFF, social studies teacher, Staples High School, Westport,
   Connecticut

PREFACE 🌿

Sharing with many people a profound disquiet about the state of the humanities in our culture, the Rockefeller Foundation decided in April 1978 to sponsor a Commission on the Humanities to assess the humanities' place and prospects. Richard W. Lyman, then president of Stanford University, agreed to chair the Commission. Its members were appointed during the summer of 1978 and met five times from September 1978 to January 1980.

The Commission was assembled fourteen years after a similar commission—sponsored by the American Council of Learned Societies, the Council of Graduate Schools in the United States, and the United Chapters of Phi Beta Kappa—had recommended the establishment of a National Humanities Foundation. The two Commissions have much in common. Both affirm the importance of the humanities and seek to heighten awareness of a national interest. Both call for continuous support of the humanities from public and private sources. Both recognize the interdependence of the humanities, social sciences, sciences, and technology. Unlike the earlier Commission, however, we do not propose the creation of a major agency. We offer a profile of the humanities in American education and public life—their contributions and weaknesses—and we recommend means for strengthening them over the next decade. Some of our thirty-one recommendations seek increases in financial support during what is sure to be a period of economic austerity. Others can be achieved with available resources. All require that we reconsider the importance of the humanities to our national culture and to the spirit of our lives.

The Commission's staff conducted research in part by communicating with educational and cultural institutions, professional associations, federal offices, commissions and task forces on issues related to the humanities, and with other groups and individuals. Our thanks go to the many who replied; the thoughtfulness of their responses reflects a broad concern for the future of the humanities. Members of the staff collected information on scores of humanistic pursuits. Although they made few site visits and did not attempt to evaluate these activities thoroughly, we have named some of the many examples that came to our attention (examples are identified in the text by a boldface dot at the beginnings of paragraphs in which they are discussed) in order to illustrate diverse forms of learning in the humanities. We decided early in our deliberations that one of the major problems of the humanities lies in the general deterioration of secondary education. We therefore called upon John Goodlad, Leroy Lovelace, and Phillip Woodruff to counsel us on matters pertaining to the schools. We are grateful to them for their eloquent advice, as we are to Richard Macksey for his reflections on the relationships among the humanities, social sciences, sciences, and technology.

We must record here with great sadness the tragic deaths, during the period of the Commission's work, of two people who were significantly connected with that work from the outset. John H. Knowles, M.D., president of the Rockefeller Foundation, died in Boston on March 6, 1979, after an illness of several weeks, at the age of fifty-two. No one who knew John Knowles's ebullience and wit, his energy and breadth of interests, and the passionate concern for human progress that he brought to his work at the Foundation can fail to mourn such a loss. Charles Frankel, Old Dominion Professor of Philosophy and Public Affairs at Columbia University and first president of the National Humanities Center in North Carolina, was a distinguished member of this Commission at the time he and his wife were murdered in May 1979 in their home in

Bedford Hills, New York. The death of Charles Frankel—philosopher, academic statesman, and public citizen—deprives the humanities of one of their most brilliant and stimulating spokesmen.

We wish to express our gratitude to the Rockefeller Foundation for its generous and constant support of this inquiry. Stanford University provided a home for our staff and extended them every courtesy. At the University of California Press, William McClung and Marilyn Schwartz edited the manuscript with insight and care. Finally, we thank Gaines Post, Jr.—associate professor of history on leave from the University of Texas at Austin—and his colleagues on the staff, Steven Young, Ellen Woods, Virginia Newton, and Donna Pinto. Theirs was the major task of putting together a report out of the great variety of materials considered and sometimes disparate views expressed.

May 9, 1980

CHAPTER ONE 🌿

The Humanities
in America

Nailed to the ship's mast in *Moby-Dick* is a gold doubloon stamped with signs and symbols "in luxuriant profusion." The coin is Captain Ahab's promised reward to the crewman who sights the white whale, but in its emblems each man reads his own meaning. As Ahab says, "This round gold is but the image of the rounder globe, which, like a magician's glass, to each and every man in turn but mirrors back his own mysterious self."

Like the bright doubloon, the humanities mirror our own image and our image of the world. Through the humanities we reflect on the fundamental question: what does it mean to be human? The humanities offer clues but never a complete answer. They reveal how people have tried to make moral, spiritual, and intellectual sense of a world in which irrationality, despair, loneliness, and death are as conspicuous as birth, friendship, hope, and reason. We learn how individuals or societies define the moral life and try to attain it, attempt to reconcile freedom and the responsibilities of citizenship, and express themselves artistically. The humanities do not necessarily mean humaneness, nor do they always inspire the individual with what Cicero called "incentives to noble action." But by awakening a sense of what it might be like to be someone else or to live in another time or culture, they tell us about ourselves, stretch our imagination, and enrich our experience. They increase our distinctively human potential.

I

The humanities presume particular methods of expression and inquiry—language, dialogue, reflection, imagination, and metaphor. In the humanities the aims of these activities of mind are not geometric proof and quantitative measure, but rather insight, perspective, critical understanding, discrimination, and creativity. These aims are not unique to the humanities, but are found in other fields, in images from the arts, and in new forms of expression created by film, television, and computers. No matter how large their circle, however, the humanities remain dedicated to the disciplined development of verbal, perceptual, and imaginative skills needed to understand experience.

For centuries the fields of knowledge most often viewed as humanistic have been languages and literatures, history, and philosophy. To these the Commission on the Humanities of 1963–64 added the arts, "the history and comparison of religion and law," and "those aspects of the social sciences which have humanistic content and employ humanistic methods." Legislation authorizing the National Endowment for the Humanities now also includes linguistics, archeology, and ethics. This Commission, too, sees languages and literatures, history, and philosophy as the central humanistic fields, and we accept these additions. But fields alone do not define the humanities:

> At their most vivid, the [humanities] are like the arts as well as the sciences. The humanities are that form of knowledge in which the knower is revealed. All knowledge becomes humanistic when this effect takes place, when we are asked to contemplate not only a proposition but the proposer, when we hear the human voice behind what is being said. (Charles Frankel, speech in Austin, Texas, December 1978)

Whether defined by questions, methods, or fields, the humanities employ a particular medium and turn of mind. The medium is language. Discourse sets in motion and supports reflection and judgment. The humanities have close ties not only with speech but especially with writing and the thought processes writing makes possible. Study in the humanistic disciplines is not limited to texts—oral cultures have reflected deeply on human experience and have achieved great wisdom—but it cannot proceed without creating and using texts. In our time the humanities necessarily have to do not only with the written word and print, but also with the electronically processed word. While the medium in the humanities is language, the turn of mind is toward history, the record of what has moved men and women before us to act, believe, and build as they did. Conscious of our links with the past, we achieve a deeper understanding of ourselves in the present and discover possibilities and limits that will shape our future.

The essence of the humanities is a spirit or an attitude toward humanity. They show how the individual is autonomous and at the same time bound, in the ligatures of language and history, to humankind across time and throughout the world. The humanities are an important measure of the values and aspirations of any society. Intensity and breadth in the perception of life and power and richness in works of the imagination betoken a people alive as moral and aesthetic beings, citizens in the fullest sense. They base their education on sustaining principles of personal enrichment and civic responsibility. They are sensitive to beauty and aware of their cultural heritage. They can approach questions of value, no matter how complex, with intelligence and goodwill. They can use their scientific and technical achievements responsibly because they see the connections among science, technology, and humanity.

This report is intended for all who care about the quality of our common life. Surveying America today, many would argue that the humanities are in crisis and would describe this crisis as symptomatic of a general weakening of our vision and resolve. Although this Commission does not take an apocalyptic view, we are deeply concerned about serious social deficiencies of perception and morale. Our society has increasingly assumed the infallibility of specialists, the necessity of regulating human activity, and the virtues of material consumption. These attitudes limit our potential to grow individually and to decide together what is for the common good. When does specialization suffocate creativity, denigrate the critical judgment of nonspecialists, or undermine the idea of leadership? When does regulation become regimentation?

At what point does materialism weaken the will to conduct our lives according to spiritual and moral values? How we as a society answer such questions will guide our activities at home and abroad. We need the humanities to help answer them intelligently and hopefully.

This Commission believes that the humanities are a social good and that their well-being is in the national interest. In this report we describe what is now being done to strengthen the humanities, and we recommend further means for invigorating them—a reconsideration of their purposes in education and public life and a mobilization of resources in their behalf. We proceed from the premise that the humanities are widely undervalued and often poorly understood.

Much of our system of education shows signs of deterioration, notably in the secondary schools. The reading and writing skills of high school seniors have declined since the early 1960s; the rate of illiteracy in this age group has been estimated at over 10 percent and as high as 20 percent. Public confidence in schooling as an institution has declined seriously since the 1960s. Tax cuts, spending limitations, and narrow applications of the "back to basics" movement result in education built on principles of management and quantitative measurement. This foundation alone cannot support the historic purposes of elementary and secondary education—discerning citizenship and personal growth—for which the humanities are essential.

Many students in schools and colleges avoid broad intellectual development in favor of acquiring immediate job skills. A national survey comparing attitudes of college freshmen in 1969 and 1979 reveals sharp declines in the importance they give to two educational objectives closely related to citizenship and individual enrichment—keeping up with political affairs and developing a philosophy of life ("The American Freshman: National Norms for Fall 1979," published early this year by the American Council on Education and the University of California at Los Angeles). Teachers of the humanities see the diminishing numbers of students in their courses as a mark of society's indifference to their work. Declining enrollments provide administrators an excuse for trimming the humanities in schools and cutting departmental budgets in colleges and universities.

The structure of higher education has cracks. In many institutions the undergraduate curriculum lacks continuity and coherence—in the humanities and in their relation to other fields. A majority of students need remedial English. Foreign language requirements for admission and graduation have been reduced or abandoned. Large numbers of graduate students and young Ph.D.'s in the humanities cannot find academic jobs; their distressing plight frightens many of the best undergraduates away from the humanities. The system of scholarly research—libraries, institutes, publishing, and sabbaticals—is jeopardized by inflation, by the even more rapid rise in the cost of materials and maintenance, and by the decline in private funding for fellowships.

From the late 1950s to the 1970s the ranks of professional humanists and academic administrators grew at an unprecedented rate. Yet in recent years many humanists and administrators have abdicated their most basic social responsibility: to help shape a philosophy of education. Some have indiscriminately applied cost-accounting methods to the curriculum without considering larger questions of educational purpose or cultural heritage. Others have dodged demands for accountability without defending the value and indeed the relevance of the humanities. Still others hold to expectations and systems of reward inherited from years of expansion, professional mobility, and self-confidence: graduate faculty, for example, have been slow to advise students about the job crisis and its implications for career and curriculum. Learned societies have failed to recognize and respond to the needs of schools, community colleges, and cultural institutions. Some educators define education narrowly according to the special needs of their institutions or the particular interests of the community. In brief, many humanists and administrators have adopted positions from which they cannot contribute to general discussion of the relationships between education, culture, and life in the community.

Efforts to define America's common culture have stirred fears among minorities that their contributions to cultural life are to be thrown back into the melting pot. The cultural debate allegedly between "elitists" and "populists" oversimplifies issues and weakens everyone's will to preserve our diverse heritage and find common values. Without widespread public commitment to cultural preservation, our museums, libraries, and other cultural institutions will have to close. Without some agreement on standards of judgment, we cannot sensitively develop new cultural forms such as television and film in which the medium is often not language and the turn of mind not historical.

Our society has only fleeting perceptions of humanism as a civic ideal. Although the humanist is above all a teacher and scholar, since ancient Athens humanists have been expected to contribute to the general sense of civic responsibility. In the middle 1960s many humanists took up the cause of civil rights, while toward the close of that decade many joined colleagues from other fields in the movement for peace in Vietnam. Not surprisingly, humanists were no more able than anyone else to resolve the battles then raging in this country over our national policies at home and abroad. As the Watergate scandal unfolded, millions wondered how supposedly educated men in our government could have such little appreciation of the requirements of civic virtue. These traumatic episodes in our recent history have done little to clarify how the humanities or indeed education can contribute to civic life through participation in and criticism of the political process.

The need to interrelate the humanities, social sciences, science, and technology has probably never been greater than today. They converge in areas such as biomedical research, the application of microprocessing and computer technologies, the conduct of government, arms control, and the safe use of natural resources—subjects requiring interdisciplinary investigation because of their social and ethical implications. Whether because of frustration, misunderstanding, or indifference, however, collaboration among humanists, scientists, and technicians is insufficient. In universities and in public life the impression persists that the humanities and sciences form two separate cultures, neither intelligible to the other. This impression indicates a fundamental kind of illiteracy.

So long as it prevails, humanists will hesitate to use new technologies, including television, to the advantage of learning. Scientists and technicians will not appreciate the relevance of the humanities. As the physical and social conditions of life change, few people will understand the real areas of interaction or divergence among science, technology, and human values.

External financial support for the humanities has increased in current dollars over the past fifteen years, thanks especially to the National Endowment for the Humanities (NEH). Created by Congress in 1965 along with the National Endowment for the Arts, the NEH has become a benefactor and representative of the humanities in Washington. But inflation and popular movements to reduce taxes have depreciated public and private support of teachers, scholars, educational institutions, libraries, and museums. The NEH itself is criticized for being either too "elitist" or too "populist" in its allocation of funds, or more generally for extending the arm of the federal bureaucracy into public (and private) life.

Many problems facing the humanities today could not have been predicted sixteen years ago when the Commission on the Humanities of 1964 issued its report. The Commission spoke of the imbalance in favor of science and technology in federal support for education and research, in curricula and enrollments, and in public opinion. This imbalance was not new, but in the years after the Soviet Union launched Sputnik it had become more visible. The members of the 1964 Commission recommended the creation of a new federal agency to bring the humanities up to the level of prestige enjoyed by the natural and social sciences. Looking beyond national borders, the Commission declared that America's world leadership could not rest merely on material wealth and advanced technology, but must also be based on "things of the spirit. If we appear to discourage creativity, to demean the fanciful and the beautiful, to have no concern for man's ultimate destiny—if, in short, we ignore the humanities—then both our goals and our efforts to attain them will be measured with suspicion" (*Report of the Commission on the Humanities*, New York, 1964).

Although few people would look back on the early 1960s as an age of American innocence, the earlier Commission's prescription for invigorating the humanities and our sense of national purpose had a straightforwardness and simplicity that can scarcely be attained today. The Commission of 1964 interpreted the problems of the arts and humanities as a lack of adequate resources. That conclusion itself has begun to seem inadequate. In seeking to go beyond the notable achievement of the earlier Commission that pointed to the creation of the two National Endowments, we are acutely conscious that, unlike our predecessor, we cannot concentrate on any single objective.

The prospects for the humanities are better than some might think. Educational opportunity in and beyond school is now available to more Americans of all origins and ages than ever before. Access to higher education has broadened in the past fifteen years as four-year institutions have expanded and two-year colleges proliferated. Total undergraduate and graduate enrollments for credit increased from about 4.8 million in 1963 to about 11.7 million in 1979; within these totals, enrollments in two-year colleges rose from about 900,000 in 1963 to 4.3 million in 1979. Noncredit enrollments in adult education have grown even more dramatically, as has public interest in the performing arts, museums, and cultural activities. The expansion and diversification of learning represent a major commitment of American democracy and have opened new possibilities for the humanities.

The exploration of these possibilities will not progress if people blame the economy for every woe. No law of history proves that minds must close when belts are tightened. We believe the humanities need reaffirmation as much as support. We see our report primarily as a contribution to rethinking the humanities, not as a shopping list. We hope that all who want to improve education and the quality of life will share this view.

DOMAINS OF THE HUMANITIES

The importance of the humanities cannot be quantified nor their needs reduced to enrollments and budgets. The humanities have no rigid institutional or intellectual boundaries. They occupy a central place in our national culture, they help shape the meaning of individuality and citizenship, and they pose fundamental questions about the human purposes of science and technology.

Culture and Citizenship

The humanities are often placed in the middle of a cultural debate that carries the shorthand description "elitism versus populism." Indeed, readers might view some arguments in this report as elitist or populist. We have not let these terms control our debate, however. We reject the elitist-populist formula as a misleading label for some real, diverse, and often confused issues in our culture.

Some people think it elitist to point out that our culture arose in what is generally described as the Western tradition; populist to affirm that Native and Latin American, African, and Asian cultures also form our heritage. Elitism is associated with high culture, which often refers to a finite list of works, authors, and standards; populism with popular culture, which has an inexhaustible list. The rich are thought elitist because they can afford educational and cultural activities the poor cannot. Those who emphasize our common culture are sometimes called elitist, whereas those who accentuate cultural pluralism are called populist. Maintaining traditional forms of cultural expression is often viewed as elitist, whereas admiring novelty and spontaneity is apparently a populist trait. It is allegedly elitist to advocate the preservation of cultural resources, populist to urge broad public access to them.

"Elitism versus populism" distorts these issues. The Western tradition includes popular culture and non-Western elements. Our common culture is not limited to the Western tradition nor restricted to the wealthy. An interpretive exhibit of Cézanne's paintings accessible to people across the country is neither elitist nor populist.

"Elitism versus populism" reduces debate to ideological categories and polarizes opinions. To be sure, the issues above express tension between cultural views that are sometimes irreconcilable and often must compete for limited resources, as we discovered in our deliberations as a Commission. Nevertheless, our discussions convinced us that we are not dealing with mutually exclusive cultural realms. Frequently the tensions can, at least in principle, be resolved. More often than not, they can generate creative energy if they are understood clearly and approached constructively.

The controversy over bilingualism exemplifies such tension. Proponents support bilingual education as the right road to full citizenship, with competence in both English and the language of origin. The President's Commission on Foreign Language and International Studies claims that denigrating the languages of immigrants and linguistic minorities has partly caused the present ignorance of foreign languages *(Strength Through Wisdom,* Washington, D.C., 1979). Critics of bilingual education, on the other hand, fear that it may create permanent foreign language enclaves in the United States, or that some children, caught halfway between two cultures, may miss opportunities or become "alingual"—not competent in any language. Congress has recently authorized the Office of Bilingual Education (Department of Education) to conduct a national evaluation of bilingual education. This study must help end the needless politicization of the issue, which prevents an acceptable resolution of the two points of view. Just last year, such politicization produced a noisy and rancorous struggle in the California State Legislature that did nothing to shed light on the genuine problems of bilingual education, still less to contribute to their solution.

American society, among the world's most diverse in its cultural origins, should cherish that diversity as a source of constantly renewed strength. But there is danger in diversity when it is carried to extremes. No society can flourish if its citizens deny the possibility of a common culture that unites all despite differences in origin, education, and outlook. This Commission does not seek to preserve a narrow set of moral, social, and aesthetic values; nor do we believe that pluralism should lead to excessive cultural particularism, crude moral relativism, or the suspension of critical judgment. We propose three principles by which the humanities can help us all find common ground amid the competing interests and values in our national life.

First, our cultural tradition contains works generally regarded as classics. This tradition holds a special regard for the past, yet is flexible and alive. Western culture has always been enlarged and enriched by non-Western cultures, by new works of art and scholarship, by the contributions of people never before given their due, and by concerns arising from our historical situation. These help define and redefine the canon of classics by forcing us to look at tradition in fresh ways.

Second, there are standards within standards. Some popular novels are more subtle than others, some Greek or Navajo myths more profound than others, some Black autobiographies more enlightening than others, some of Shakespeare's plays more effective dramatically than others. It is in no way undemocratic to recognize these distinctions, and only confusion and bigotry gain by denying them. All people have the capacity to reach for high standards of expression, interpretation, and discrimination; these are not exclusive privileges of one class or culture.

Third, education has a socializing dimension, as individuals share ideas, relate particular experiences to universal concerns, sharpen their moral faculties, and serve the community. The humanities, by emphasizing our common humanity, contribute especially to the social purpose of learning—to education for civic participation, which has been a strong theme in American society since the days of Thomas Jefferson.

No conception of the humanities is complete if it omits humanism as a civic ideal. In the European Renaissance many humanists connected learning with civic duty and decried what they took to be the pedantic, unworldly attitudes of medieval scholasticism. Since the Renaissance the connections between education and public life have multiplied. Democracy rests on the principle of enlightened self-rule by the entire citizenry. So, in a sense, does our modern system of cultural patronage. In the Renaissance the humanities depended on a few patrons; today support for and participation in the humanities are public forces and public responsibilities on a large scale. Finally, though slowly, the meaning of cosmopolitanism has broadened, and with it the idea of citizenship. We cannot afford to look parochially at other cultures as curiosities, "like us" only insofar as their members have converted to Christianity or studied at Oxford or Yale.

These important social changes do not point to a simple or

single ideal of civic virtue. Our republic stands on a belief that educated citizens will participate effectively in decisions concerning the whole community. Humanistic education helps prepare individuals for this civic activity. The humanities lead beyond "functional" literacy and basic skills to critical judgment and discrimination, enabling citizens to view political issues from an informed perspective. Through familiarity with foreign cultures—as well as with our own subcultures—the humanities show that citizenship means belonging to something larger than neighborhood or nation. Complementing the political side of citizenship is the cultural. A literate public does not passively receive cultural works from academic guardians, but actively engages in the interpretation, creation, and re-creation of those works. Participation in the republic of letters is participation in community life as well.

Although the humanities pertain to citizenship, they also have an integrity of their own. They are not always relevant to urgent social or political issues. They are not simply a means to advanced literacy or cultivation. Nor are they a duty, a requirement, or a kind of finishing-school concern—froth on the brew, embroidery on the blanket. If to grow in wisdom—not simply in cleverness, or dexterity, or learning—is practical, then the humanities, properly conceived and conveyed, are decidedly practical. They help develop capacities hard to define clearly and without cliché: a sharpened critical judgment, a keener appreciation of experience. Study of the humanities makes distinctive marks on the mind: through history, the ability to disentangle and interpret complex human events; through literature and the arts, the ability to distinguish the deeply felt, the well wrought, and the continually engrossing from the shallow, the imitative, and the monotonous; through philosophy, the sharpening of criteria for moral decision and warrantable belief.

These capacities serve much more than the notion that, as a member of a community or state, the individual has civic duties and virtues. There are other values besides civic ones, and they are often found in privacy, intimacy, and distance from civic life. The humanities sustain this second conception of individuality, as deeply rooted as the other in our cultural inheritance, in three important ways. First, they emphasize the individual's critical vigilance over political activity. This is a form of civic participation, but it demands judgment acquired through detachment and circumspection. Second, teaching and scholarship in the humanities frequently consider subjects beyond those of immediate public concern; the humanities pursue matters of value without defining value as social utility. Finally, the humanities offer intensely personal insights into the recesses of experience. Ultimately, the individual interprets what appears in the gold doubloon.

The humanities illuminate relationships between the public and private notions of individuality. The two sometimes reinforce each other, sometimes remain indifferent to each other. They often pull away from each other, and are at times irreparably divided.

Science and Technology

Affinity and tension also exist between the humanities and science and technology. Their interconnections have been obscured by an oversimplified thesis of conflict between the humanistic and the scientific, a misperception that diminishes both. It is particularly inappropriate when many humanists are turning to computer technology for the exploration of practical problems and to scientific models for insight into such questions as the structure of language and the nature of thought. Correspondingly, when scientists and technicians are deeply concered about questions raised by their unprecedented success in transforming the human environment, when questions of value, responsibility, and freedom can no longer be seen as falling outside the province of scientific activity, dialogue with humanists becomes increasingly important.

While this Commission does not minimize the uncertainties implicit in science and technology, we want to underscore their creative connections with and potentials for the humanities. New informational technologies can relieve humanistic inquiry of many routine burdens. They and scientific models can sharpen perceptions in many fields of knowledge and give insights into the characteristics of information. Social and ethical questions are intrinsic to science and technology. In these respects science and technology have been a domain of the humanities in Western culture since its Greek origins.

For many centuries literature and public discourse have viewed technology ambivalently, as both curse and cure. In Plato's *Phaedrus*, Socrates feared that writing would destroy memory and wisdom by enabling people to compile quantities of lifeless information. Similar apprehensions underlay denunciations of printing in the sixteenth century, closely paralleling the alarms expressed today about microprocessing and computer technologies. Writing, printing, and computing all represent technological revolutions in disseminating information. All had or have profound implications for social change. The last of these technologies, if intelligently used, may be as beneficial to the humanities as the other two have been.

The revolution in telecommunications and data processing is transforming the way knowledge is gathered, stored, and transmitted. The magnitude of this revolution is still only dimly perceived. The speed with which information can reach an individual and the quantity of information that can be electronically stored have multiplied more than a thousandfold in the past two decades. Through advances in microprocessing, each major informational technology—telephone, computer, and television—is becoming increasingly sophisticated. Each grows compatible with the others and with related technologies. New and coupled technologies can help students, teachers, scholars, and adult learners by saving time and offering versatile modes of learning. The new technologies provide libraries and other institutions with indispensable means for preserving and storing materials and for increasing access to them.

The new informational technologies take us beyond quantities of information to some of the processes of human intelligence. Techniques of microprocessing have been used to measure and improve perception, logic, conceptualization, and language. For example, computers and visual displays enable one to conceptualize forms that can be judged aesthetically, as in mathematical equations and architectural design.

To explore this cognitive terrain wisely, humanists, scientists, and technicians must overcome divisions that have been institutionalized in our educational system. They have grown accustomed to working separately. Many assume that their methods are as alien as their respective corners of the campus. On the other hand, some humanists have been too easily seduced by scientific mannerisms without genuine insight into scientific methods, and some scientists and engineers have turned to humanists for premature resolutions of ethical or interpretive dilemmas without the patience to observe how humanists formulate questions or manage inquiry.

Between the extremes of unnatural isolation and uncritical coalescence, debate must animate classrooms, colloquia, institutes, publications, and public forums. Differences will surface. The humanist, usually oriented toward the study of the past, serves as an articulated cultural memory. The scientist and technician, primarily oriented toward the present and future, look at what is given in and expected of the natural order. The humanist often proceeds by progressively inclusionary acts that make the precise field of inquiry hard to fix. The scientist and technician normally proceed through a series of systematic exclusions toward precise proofs and laws. The humanistic method is usually allusive and interrogative, whereas the scientific is experimental and declarative. Humanists may have developed a more sophisticated conception of criticism than have scientists, yet they may fall behind the latter in defining standards of error.

These distinctions are not irreconcilable. They contain more promise for collaboration than for antagonism. Lord Bullock has described the humanities as having links to both the sciences and the arts—"to reason, logic, and the systematic procedures of scholarship on one side; to the insights of imagination, intuition, emotion, and fantasy on the other." The humanities are "a mixed economy in which there are to be found, side by side, elements of fact, speculation and judgment, the objective and the subjective" ("The Future of Humanistic Studies," lecture presented at the Aspen Institute, Summer 1978). As a "mixed economy" the humanities are able to adapt to congenial methods or assumptions in science and technology and also in the social sciences, where perhaps the humanities and the natural sciences most overlap. At the same time, the humanities help discern where these other broad fields of knowledge lose touch with human values.

This Commission need not elaborate the fact that throughout history science and technology have had enormous impact on the way people work, live, and die. In the latter part of the twentieth century, war is not the only major moral dilemma nor genocide the only agent of dehumanization. Urgent ethical and social questions are being raised in the behavioral sciences and in areas of biomedicine such as experimentation with human subjects, genetic engineering and behavior control, human reproduction, and the termination of life. Technology has generated extraordinary demands on space, energy, and natural resources. The resulting questions about pollution and about constraints on growth are essentially ethical and aesthetic. Communications technology raises ethical and social issues such as the already visible tendency to model expectations for human behavior on the capacities of computers.

Many scientists and technicians have recognized the urgent need for cooperative study of the relationships among science, technology, and values. Especially since the Second World War, they have been concerned about their social and moral responsibilities, about how their activities as a group impinge on a larger community. Today the feeling is stronger than ever before that the construction of technological devices cannot be justified without regard for the consequences. Scientists in turn are troubled by the fact that as agents of unprecedented power they are not themselves philosophers or trained arbiters of value; and they rightly suspect that those who allow social predilections to influence technical judgments may end up with science that is bad as well as dangerous. To be a good scientist one must be more than a scientific specialist.

How then can scientists and technicians live up to their human responsibilities and make intelligent decisions about moral, social, and other human values that are related to their professional performance? There have been two characteristic responses to this dilemma. The first maintains that the scientist as scientist need only be concerned with the search for verifiable truth and that the technician as technician need only pursue the technical goals of a particular profession, but that both are human beings and must therefore help to decide the social goals that science and technology finally serve. Since most discoveries in science and developments in technology can be used for ends that are either good or evil, scientists and technicians must assume social responsibility for the consequences of their work. In this view, they do so in their capacities as human beings rather than as scientists or technicians: their responsibilities are neither greater than nor different from those of the laity. In short, matters of value are not relevant to science and technology as such.

The second and opposing argument maintains that science and technology inevitably embody a system of values for which their practitioners are uniquely responsible. In this view, the scientist as scientist and the technician as technician are more than licensed professionals, whether or not they admit this to themselves. They work in a value-laden context; their professional involvement is predicated upon values it preserves as well as presupposes. They are therefore responsible not only as human beings who must decide how their powers are to be used, but also as creative individuals who can foresee the social consequences of their work and must act accordingly. They have a privilege in judging how present activities determine future effects.

Summarized in this way, both positions may be extreme. Still, the question of personal and professional responsibility was acute for German scientists during the Nazi regime, when the German university's achievements in research were so impressive and the cause in which this research was enlisted was so appalling.

Faced with the same fundamental question today, some scientists have turned to humanists—particularly philosophers—for expert guidance. They have too often come away disappointed. They think of philosophy as, quite literally, the love of wisdom; and therefore they are shocked to find that philosophers and other humanists generally disavow having access to special or eternal truths. The scientists' disappointment stems from two opposite misapprehensions: expecting too much of humanists and expecting too little. Scientists and technicians expect too much if they think any humanist, even the wisest, can serve as an ultimate authority liberating others from the necessity of deliberating about ethical problems. We note this tendency in the National Science Foundation (Office of Science and Society), which seems to expect humanist participants in certain projects to act as "experts" who solve vexing problems of public policy. On the other hand, scientists and technicians are also mistaken if they fail to realize that the humanities can provide useful conceptual and analytical tools for examining concrete human problems.

The application of the humanities to scientific and technological problems must always remain tentative, partly because humanists disagree among themselves and partly because in questions of value each person is largely autonomous. But the able humanist can awaken scientists and technicians to problems of which they may not have been aware, pose analytical distinctions of a unique sort, and point to the boundaries beyond which civilized societies have agreed that human dignity is in peril.

The guidelines of both the National Science Foundation and the National Endowment for the Humanities recognize the merging of the scientific and the humanistic in questions of value. Yet both agencies remain timid in expanding this area of common interest; both fall back on exclusionary definitions of what is scientific or humanistic. They must find ways to take advantage of the fact that humanists have allies in science, technology, and the social sciences. In collaboration, people from these fields can mitigate some of the educational and public harm done by widespread acceptance of the thesis that two cultures—one scientific and technical, the other humanistic—cannot be bridged.

The human purposes of science and technology impose obligations on all educators. Our citizens need to become literate in a multiple sense. We all need to understand the characteristics of scientific inquiry and the repercussions of scientific research. We must all learn something about the use of the media and of new technologies for storing, transmitting, and expanding knowledge. Without this sort of literacy, our society as a whole will be less able to apply science and technology to humanistic needs, less able to measure the human effects of scientific achievements, less able to judge the information we produce and receive. Our schools and colleges have no higher duty than to sharpen these critical senses, which are inseparable from the humanities.

PRIORITIES AND RECOMMENDATIONS

Our recommendations are intended for many audiences: administrators, faculty, and students; state legislatures and departments of education; Congress and federal agencies; cultural institutions; the media; private foundations and corporations; the general public. They will find three types of recommendations. First, we ask for major increases in resources for elementary and secondary education (chapter two), for research (chapter three), and for operating expenses of cultural institutions (chapter four). We consider these top national priorities for support in the 1980s. Second, we propose measures, especially in post-secondary curricula and interpretive programs outside higher education, that can be implemented by reallocating available resources, though in some cases additional support from external sources will be necessary. Third, we make recommendations—and indeed develop themes in the report—that have no direct financial implications. These relate chiefly to perceptions of education and culture.

Each recommendation requires change and choice. From what current attitudes or practices, to and between what necessities, and to what degree: the decisions will vary according to the audience. Our own meetings have confirmed how difficult it is for any committee to discuss the humanities. Our meetings have also brought us to this consensus: the humanities are a vital national resource, inexhaustible because they come from mind and spirit, yet perishable through neglect.

Priorities for the 1980s

We see seven major needs for American education and cultural life in the 1980s. The first three we have already mentioned as national priorities requiring financial support for the humanities. The remaining four are themes throughout the report, each a necessity for the future.

1. *The highest priority is to improve the quality of education in our elementary and secondary schools.* Our schools must prepare young people for competent and informed participation in community life and for the greatest possible degree of fulfillment in private life. These are not possible without the humanities. Through the humanities one acquires not only literacy but conceptual, critical, and aesthetic capacities as basic as literacy itself. One learns to value cultural tradition and change, active citizenship and private contemplation. Our society must not deprive its children of this educational foundation as the average age of the population increases and many institutions become preoccupied with the needs of adults.

2. *Research in the humanities must be supported.* Advanced training and research, though not necessarily applicable to immediate public issues, are as necessary for the humanities as for the sciences. In humanistic disciplines scholars usually work without complicated apparatus and their discoveries seldom attract public fanfare—realities that have always hindered broad understanding of the importance of humanistic scholarship. Yet without scholarship the analysis and reinterpretation of our cultural traditions will languish and education in the humanities will atrophy. Given the inroads of inflation, the financial needs of fellowships, libraries, archives, research institutes, and publishing—interrelated parts of scholarship—far exceed available funds, public and private.

3. *Our cultural institutions must receive sufficient funds for their preservative and educational missions.* For museums, libraries, and historical societies, the combined costs of conservation, maintenance, security, acquisitions, and interpretive programs have increased faster than inflation. Public support for these institutions must refute the erroneous argument that they do not provide essential community services for which taxes ought to pay. Federal and private sources of support should not compound the financial difficulties of cultural institutions by distinguishing between operating expenses and programs and markedly preferring to fund the latter. Sources of support as well as cultural institu-

tions themselves should view programs as normal and necessary operations.

4. *Educators must reaffirm the value of the humanities.* The greatest challenge for the humanities is not to increase enrollments or support but to demonstrate their contribution to education and public life. Administrators and humanists must assert that essential goals of education depend on the humanities—the development of citizens who can make informed and critical judgments, and the enrichment of individual life. Administrators must reward efforts by humanists to be mediators: in the curriculum, between the humanities and the vocational and personal interests of students; in lifelong learning, between educational and cultural institutions and the media, and between institutions and the public; in community life, between scholarship and contemporary concerns.

5. *Educational and cultural institutions and sources of support for the humanities must collaborate.* We emphasize the need for collaboration for intellectual and financial reasons. The questions raised by the humanities and the basic methods they employ cross institutional lines, public and private, and belong to every generation. Cooperation can lead to more efficient use of the limited available resources.

6. *The terms of cultural debate need to be clarified.* The humanities cannot be accurately described in terms of elitism and populism. To recognize the importance of classics in all cultural traditions is not to deny the creative interplay of tradition and reevaluation. Preserving cultural institutions is compatible with interpreting their collections for large and diverse audiences. When the humanities do not relate directly to contemporary public issues or draw large crowds, the reason should be sought in the private and detached qualities of some humanistic inquiry rather than in its alleged irrelevance.

7. *The humanities, sciences, and technology need to be substantially connected.* People can use the humanities to reach judgments about questions that may seem to be chiefly scientific or technical but really depend for answers on ethics, traditions, sensibilities, and values. Our educational institutions must cultivate a literacy that enables everyone to view technology rationally and to understand

the broad dimensions of scientific inquiry. The humanities should use media and informational technologies more than they now do.

Summary of Recommendations

Our report includes recommendations for strengthening the humanities in the schools, higher education, and continuing or nonformal education. Wherever possible, we have suggested who should implement our recommendations. Often we propose a shared responsibility because we believe that the humanities' best hope for the future lies in collaboration among many individuals and institutions. The following summary previews what readers will find in chapters two through five.

Elementary and secondary schools need leaders at the local, state, and federal levels to set goals that embody America's high educational ideals. The importance of the humanities in achieving those goals goes beyond the narrow range of accomplishment measured by proficiency tests for students and certification requirements for teachers. Educational policy makers at all levels should define critical thinking as a basic skill and recognize the value of the humanities for developing it. The National Endowment for the Humanities needs to advance public discussion of the purposes of education. Federal agencies and state boards of education must promote exemplary programs in the humanities that integrate expository, analytical, and aesthetic skills with knowledge of cultural traditions, technology, and science. Government agencies, private foundations, and learned societies can help improve the competence and status of teachers of the humanities through programs of professional development and recognition. States, colleges, and universities must insure that teachers' education includes solid preparation in the humanities and liberal arts. Colleges, universities, museums, and public libraries should collaborate with local schools to use existing resources in improving education in the humanities.

Colleges and universities must underscore the importance of the humanities in undergraduate education and in graduate education for the professions. In restoring the ideals of liberal education to undergraduate learning, educators should emphasize the value of the humanities for effective self-expression; for enjoyment and judgment of the arts; for understanding other cultures; and for assessment of ethical problems, issues of public policy, and questions of value raised by science and technology. Strategies for strengthening the curriculum include continuous instruction in writing, interdisciplinary courses, clear sequences of courses in the humanities, and cooperation with local cultural institutions. Medical schools, business schools, and other professional schools all benefit if their applicants and graduates have solid training in the humanities. Graduate programs in the humanities need to adapt thoughtfully to patterns of academic and non-academic employment. Public and private sources of funds must increase their support for research in the humanities.

Educational institutions, museums, libraries, historical organizations, and the media can stimulate public learning in the humanities. Humanists can help develop programs offered to the public by educational and cultural institutions and the media, and academic administrators should reward such faculty activities. Colleges and universities will enrich vocational courses, adult basic education, and extension curricula by incorporating the humanities in them. Museums, libraries, and historical organizations can combine their preservative and educational functions through interpretive exhibits that make their resources in the humanities accessible to the public. Public and private sources of support for cultural institutions must increase funds for the general operating expenses of these institutions. A general assessment of national policy for cultural preservation is needed.

Sources of support for the humanities will find, throughout our report, suggestions for focusing their funding efforts. All sources, from state legislatures to private philanthropy, should recognize the fundamental contributions of the humanities to the quality of American life. Many sources (particularly foundations and corporations) may need to review best uses of the support they already provide or can provide for the humanities. They should examine their policies with a view to sustaining successful programs and increasing support for elementary and secondary education, research, and the operating expenses of institutions.

Public and private sources should collaborate in identifying priorities for funding, collecting information on current patterns of support, and assessing the relationship between federal and private support and the impact of both on the field of applicants.

We join a succession of commissions and citizens' groups in urging that corporations use more fully the 5 percent of pretax income the law allows them to deduct for charitable contributions; they should also increase the portion of these contributions to the humanities. Congress should increase the program budget of the NEH at a rate that at least keeps pace with inflation, and gradually raise the ceilings on Challenge Grants and matching funds. Although the record of the NEH is commendable, we believe that the agency has neglected elementary and secondary education. With guidance from the National Council on the Humanities, the Endowment should clarify its policies of support in ways that transcend divisive ideological terms.

CHAPTER TWO 🌿

The Humanities
in the Schools

A dramatic improvement in the quality of education in our elementary and secondary schools is the highest educational priority for America in the 1980s.

Our public schools are the only means for attaining the extraordinary ideal envisioned by Thomas Jefferson: a system of public education that prepares all young men and women for participation in a democratic society. This ideal, though surely no monopoly of the humanist, cannot be achieved without education in the humanities. Although we emphasize public schools in this report—they enroll about 90 percent of all students—we recognize that private schools are a valuable national resource, are often strongly dedicated to the humanities, and frequently interact with public education through students and faculty who transfer from one sector to the other. We hope that some of our recommendations will help private schools sustain and strengthen their programs in the humanities.

The Commission on the Humanities of 1964 underlined the importance of the schools, adding to their main report an appendix, "The Humanities and the Schools." They made general recommendations for improving the humanities in elementary and secondary education and concluded, with cautious optimism: "The task before us in the humanities is no overnight job. For the ills of our schools there is no quick cure. But there is no reason for dismay or delay" (*Report of the Commission on the Humanities*, New York, 1964).

There has been delay, and there is now ample reason for dismay.

There is alarming evidence of lowered levels of academic achievement among high school graduates and of school practices that condone low standards. A 1977 survey reported that 13 percent of all the seventeen-year-olds studied were illiterate (Education Commission of the States, *National Assessment of Educational Progress*, Washington, D.C.). More recently, a paper prepared for the National Commission on Libraries and Information Science estimated that one out of five high school seniors is unable to carry out everyday reading tasks upon graduation ("Theme Conference on Libraries and Literacy," Washington, D.C., 1979). Illiteracy is at the low end of a general decline along the entire scale of academic achievement after grade four. Although achievement has improved in the primary grades over the past fifteen years, falling scores on standardized tests administered to grades five through twelve have reinforced the testimony of employers and colleges that young people cannot read and write adequately. The failures of students point to compromises in the schools. "Grade inflation," reduced homework, textbooks "written down" to easier levels of language proficiency: these practices have placed fewer and smaller demands on students to meet acceptable standards of academic achievement.

The failures of students and schools can be related to larger social problems that the nation has not solved. Drugs and violence in the hallways of some of our schools have impeded learning. So, in some respects, has the growth of the electronic media. Absenteeism is widespread, and in some urban schools dropout rates run as high as 45 percent. Faith in the power of education to open doors to opportunity has been shaken by inflation and unemployment, and by evidence that class, race, and sex may be the chief determinants of economic success.

Such deficiencies taken together have contributed to a potentially disastrous loss of confidence in schooling as an institution.

The decline of popular support, documented in national polls of the Gallup organization and the National Center for Education Statistics, probably results partly from changing demographic patterns. As population growth has leveled off and the median age of Americans has risen, school enrollments have decreased and the number of adults having any immediate contact with local schools has diminished. It is not unusual to find communities in which fewer than one of every four adults is directly concerned with the schools.

The fading of public confidence, however, goes beyond indifference. It is part of a general loss of confidence in American political and social institutions—Congress, industry, the courts, federal and local civil services. For reasons that are not always related to education, many Americans, including parents of school-age children, support proposals that threaten to undermine the most democratic educational system in the world. Tax reductions, limitations on spending, tuition tax credits, and educational voucher systems further reduce financial resources already diminished by the falling birth rate. Additional revenue is lost when parents withdraw their children from public schools out of dissatisfaction with the quality of public education.

Although they doubt that the schools can—or should—cure the nation's social ills, Americans still believe that education has more than economic value. Yet few people pause to consider the consequences of reducing the resources of our public schools. Indeed, few circles are more clearly vicious: declining support exacerbates the day-to-day problems of large classes, heavy teaching loads, limited library collections, and the threat of layoffs and school closings; and these in turn contribute to further erosion of public confidence. Thus when the schools find themselves in a crossfire of demands—from federal and state governments, from the courts, from parents who censor books or oppose racial integration, and from special interest groups advocating narrow educational priorities—they find no general base of support on which they can rely. Amid such pressures there can be little consensus on what ought to be taught, and why.

It is much easier to criticize our schools than to acknowledge their conscientious efforts to provide young people a substantial education based on sound principles. In this chapter we shall cite examples of such efforts, which demonstrate that the humanities can and must form a major part of the basic education of all Americans.

A popular response to the high rate of illiteracy among high school graduates, the "back to basics" movement marks a return to the utilitarian tradition in American education, according to which students are expected to master the practical skills necessary for work and basic social discourse. For the humanities, "back to basics" is a mixed blessing. Improving the reading and writing skills of students is a goal of and a foundation for study in the humanities. But wherever basic education concentrates exclusively on the three R's, or whenever academic achievement is reduced to what can be measured by standardized testing, the humanities are likely to be misunderstood as expendable frills. The notion that the humanities improve the mind, nurture the spirit, and inform moral and civic choices can be all but lost in the rush "back to basics."

To reject or ignore the humanities in the name of literacy would be a tragic mistake. Americans have traditionally set loftier goals for education than the acquisition of basic skills alone, and simply eliminating illiteracy will not restore public confidence in the schools. A free society depends on citizens who are broadly educated. The humanities form a bridge between functional literacy and the higher intellectual and civic purposes of learning. Study of the humanities is also a personal kind of learning, answering a need that grows out of particular experience. Whatever a student's background, the humanities help clarify questions of moral, social, and aesthetic value that each individual encounters throughout learning and life. By showing young people how others have searched for meaning in their lives, the humanities help them think critically about themselves and their place in the world.

In acquiring skills in native and foreign languages, students learn logic, classification, and comparison. These conceptual skills are no less basic than literacy itself. They enable young people to go beyond merely functional tasks to wonder, imagine, and decide what is good, what is enjoyable, how their lives should be lived. The arts, companions to the humanities, awaken young people to the possibilities of human expression, sharpen their senses, and introduce them to cultural traditions through study of—and participation in—literature, music, the visual arts, theater, and dance. Students grow sensitive to the expressive possibilities of beauty and form and to the ways artists represent human experience and encounter aesthetic problems. Education in the arts is more than a sampling of "great works" or modes of self-expression. It also helps students sense the aesthetic dimensions of their everyday lives.

Education in the humanities requires factual knowledge of ideas, values, and tastes. Without such knowledge the world's cultural traditions cannot be understood; without it attempts at critical discussion become pointless. To many people an insistence on facts smacks of rote learning. Nothing could be farther from our aim. Effective instruction in the humanities encourages a creative interplay of fact and imagination.

Because each generation views the factual basis of the humanities from a new vantage point, education in the humanities should focus on major themes common to human experience rather than adhere to a rigid canon of "great works." Yet some works have been so important in shaping our cultural heritage that it is foolish to ignore them in the classroom or omit them from the shelves of school libraries. All young people should be introduced to classics from the Western cultural tradition, foreign cultures, and American racial and ethnic groups. In selecting appropriate works and teaching them, teachers must be sensitive to the age, background, and capacities of individual students. Much can be gained by repetition: reconsidering works first encountered at an earlier stage of learning gives rise to new insights and contributes to a gratifying sense of personal achievement.

By developing conceptual skills and imparting knowledge of traditions, the humanities encourage a critical examination of human values. To be sure, the capacity to discriminate and judge is a central goal of all education. But the humanities have a special critical function. Just as students must learn to manage quantifiable fact and error through the study of mathematics and the natural sciences, they must also learn how to discriminate good from bad in matters of human action, choice, and belief. In these domains, the evidence is often ambiguous. The humanities do not impose any single set of normative values, whether moral, social, or aesthetic; rather, as a record of the ideals that have guided men and women in the past, they give historical perspective. Students made sensitive to what it might be like to live in a different time, place, or culture can make value choices without automatically assuming that contemporary reality has no precedent, or that quick scientific or humanistic prescriptions can remedy every problem. The humanities bring to life the ideal of cultural pluralism by expanding the number of perspectives from which questions of value may be viewed, by enlarging young people's social and historical consciousness, and by activating an imaginative critical spirit.

Their critical approach to value choices does not put the humanities at odds with the traditional social mission of American schools—preparing students for citizenship by teaching the democratic values that have shaped the American heritage. For learning to be critical does not imply disloyalty to traditional values. Indeed, questioning, debate, and dissent are central to our heritage. They leaven the stable values of citizenship— charity, tolerance, and goodwill—that ennoble the American definition of civic virtue.

Many young people today lack confidence in the future, their precocious cynicism reflecting our failure to solve persistent social problems and our growing awareness of limited material resources. In times of economic uncertainty, young people are often urged to prepare for earning a livelihood and discouraged from studying the humanities. We can ill afford to starve the spirit that moves each younger generation to search for humane solutions to perennial human problems and unprecedented ones alike. The humanities contain that spirit. In the humanities our children will find examples of courage and resilience in the face of moral challenge or technological change. Through the humanities they can develop capacities for judgment and discrimination, as well as the curiosity and imagination to go beyond what has been thought, said, and done before: basic skills for the creation of a future.

Our educational system is extraordinarily complex and diverse, with over sixteen thousand school districts and some ninety thousand public schools, as well as thousands of private institutions. Therefore, we direct our recommendations to major sources of policy making and support, which share responsibility for improving the humanities in elementary and secondary education.

EDUCATIONAL POLICY

Authority over educational policy is divided unequally among federal, state, and local levels of jurisdiction. Although the federal presence has expanded since the passage of the Elementary and Secondary Education Act (ESEA) in 1965, generally state legislatures and departments of education determine school policy, and local school districts decide how they will implement state and federal policy. The heaviest responsibility for improving the quality of education falls upon local school boards, superintendents, and others who allocate resources. People at the local level must inform and respond to state and federal policy so as to emphasize the relationship between a good education and the humanities.

RECOMMENDATION 1: Local school board members and superintendents of schools must establish the humanities as a priority in the curriculum of their districts. To supplement their own resources in the humanities, school districts should maintain an active file of exemplary programs and possible sources of support.

The diversity of America's schools is a national strength to which both public and many kinds of privately funded schools have contributed. For this reason we do not recommend one policy or approach for all. Nor do we advise schools to imitate programs that have been successful elsewhere without carefully adapting them to the distinctive local setting. We hope this report will stimulate discussion among school boards, superintendents, principals, curriculum supervisors, and teachers. They must reject the notion that the humanities and arts are "soft" and instead view them as part of a basic education, linking literacy to cognitive, aesthetic, and critical skills. We call upon all local schools to uphold the value of the humanities for individual enrichment and civic participation.

Because the quality of elementary and secondary education is an issue for the entire community, school districts must help increase public awareness of what a good education means and how much it costs. They must use resources found inside and outside their borders—including private organizations, state and federal departments of education, and the National Endowment for the Humanities—which support programs, their dissemination, and public forums. The State Humanities Committees (or Councils), which are supported by the Endowment but make grants independently, may be particularly responsive to the needs of school districts within each state. A reciprocal obligation to provide guidance concerning the humanities exists between people at the district level and their respective professional associations, such as the National School Boards Association, National Association of Elementary School Principals, National Association of Secondary School Principals, Association for Supervision and Curriculum Development, American Association of School Administrators, American Federation of Teachers, National Education Association, and the disciplinary associations. In addition, school districts should tap the resources of institutions discussed later in this report—colleges and universities, museums, libraries, historical societies, and the media. Finally, because state regulations establish guidelines for local decisions about curriculum and instruction, local education officials should advise higher authorities on how state and federal policy affect the humanities.

RECOMMENDATION 2:   States must establish funding policies and other guidelines enabling schools to provide all students with a general education that includes significant attention to the humanities. State education officials should enlist the best teachers available to help them defend the immeasurable educational value of the questions, methods, and fields of the humanities. The makers of state policy must not shortchange educational goals that resist quantification.

The public conception of educational goals is broad and philosophical. Preliminary analysis of the findings of the comprehensive Study of Schooling in the United States, conducted by the Institute for the Development of Educational Activities (IDEA) in Los Angeles, shows that many parents, students, and teachers expect schools to stress each of the four traditional sets of goals for schooling: intellectual or academic, vocational, social (including especially the meaning of citizenship), and personal (including emotional and aesthetic development). In a recent survey taken by the Wisconsin Department of Public Instruction, respondents ranked highest in importance the need for high school graduates to be able to accept responsibility. Thinking, citizenship, and responsibility are not adequately measured by proficiency tests or taught simply by adding more subjects to the curriculum.

Most states now require proficiency tests; a few require them for graduation from high school, and some are developing them for promotion from one grade to the next. While their long-range impact on student achievement has yet to be determined, these tests have clearly succeeded in mobilizing school and community resources around the problem of illiteracy. They provide educators with hard evidence needed to satisfy public demands for accountability. But the narrow range of skills and knowledge measured by most competency testing should not define, much less be equated with, the goals of education. Legislators should recognize that when they endorse minimum standards of competency they in fact endorse a maximum education for many students, especially those in vocational "tracks" who do not pursue an academic course of study. When the main goal of students is to pass a test, teachers tend to "teach for the test." State policy can reinforce a mechanical approach to learning.

Most states also require schools to include certain subjects in the curriculum. These requirements guide schools on the relative priority of various subjects and thus indicate to parents and students what is important about education. The number of mandated subjects has increased over the past two decades, in about twenty states to over twenty subjects, largely in response to the pressure of special interest groups on national and state policy. We profoundly regret that this trend has caused fundamental subjects such as history, English, art, and foreign languages to lose ground.

When political debates concentrate on the narrow concerns of specific groups, state legislators should recall the following corrective principle that applies to all citizens: a good and challenging education develops the qualities of mind and spirit necessary for living up to one's potential as a thoughtful person and active citizen. State superintendents, boards, and departments of education must uphold this principle when they make decisions about testing, curriculum, certification, textbook adoption, library resources, staff development, student attendance, and the allocation of funds. To discuss these issues—as well as the need for collaboration between schools and colleges—we urge that a group such as the American Association for the Advancement of the Humanities arrange a conference on education in the humanities for representatives from the fifty states.

RECOMMENDATION 3:   The federal Department of Education and the National Endowment for the Humanities (NEH) should make more effective use of their distinctive capacities for strengthening the humanities in the nation's schools. While funding and control of elementary and secondary education occur at the local and state levels, federal initiatives influence state and local agencies in setting educational priorities. A firm federal commitment to the humanities can thus be multiplied many times over as it spreads through the system of public education. Specifically:
   —The new Department of Education, in its efforts to extend educational opportunity, should see that all American children have access to a *good* education. Billion-dollar federal programs for the educationally deprived, especially

at the secondary level, should recognize the importance
of the humanities in the development of conceptual and
critical skills necessary for the fullest exercise of individual
rights.

— The NEH ought to make its programs better known to local
school districts in an effort to improve curriculum and
instruction. Through its Public, State, and Special Programs,
the Endowment should energetically promote public discussion of the purposes and needs of elementary and
secondary education.

— The NEH and the Department of Education must improve
their efforts to disseminate exemplary programs so that
successful models of education in the humanities reach the
local level. We strongly recommend that the Education
Division of the NEH remain an independent resource and
not be incorporated in the new Department.

The report of the Humanities Commission of 1964 emphasized that improving the teaching of the humanities in the schools
should be a high national priority. In 1965 the National Foundation on the Arts and Humanities Act assigned joint responsibility
for strengthening education in the arts and humanities to the two
new Endowments and the Office of Education (OE). But neither
OE nor the NEH has lived up to the expectations raised by these
two documents.

In the late 1960s the Office of Education sponsored teachers'
institutes in the humanistic disciplines and projects such as
Artists-in-Schools. Though references to OE were removed from
the reauthorization legislation of the National Foundation (1973),
OE maintained an Arts and Humanities Office (with emphasis on
the arts) and continued to provide some support for projects
related to the humanities. But the humanities are a small pebble on
a large beach. The primary mission of OE, according to its
proposed budget for fiscal year (FY) 1980, has been "to assure that
all Americans have equal access to a good education." Of the $6.8
billion for elementary and secondary education in 1980, less than 4
percent (about $263 million) is designated as funding that might
cover programs in the humanities or arts: $117 million for special

projects and training to support "the pursuit of excellence" in schools and communities, including Teacher Corps and Teacher Centers; and $146 million in Support and Innovation Grants to states for improving local educational practices (ESEA Title IV-C). Even here the humanities compete with many other subjects and receive only a small fraction of available funds. (Though some categories of appropriation have been reorganized in the Department of Education, with School Improvement Programs taking over a number of activities formerly known as special projects and training, the proposed budget for FY1981 maintains similar portions of funds available for the humanities.)

The Department of Education should preserve the twofold mission of access and quality that it inherits from OE, and we support its efforts to serve Americans who have too long been neglected by the educational system. The aim of most ESEA Title I programs—$3.5 billion in FY1980—is to bring disadvantaged students up to a minimally acceptable level of language skills. The Right to Read program—now expanded into the Basic Skills Improvement program with a budget of $35 million for FY1980— is a profound democratic mandate. However, the legislative language and goals of these programs, and the types of projects funded by them, point to a narrow and quantitative definition of compensatory education and basic skills. This definition implicitly excludes the humanities beyond the bare minimum of literacy. Literacy is the foundation for learning at every stage of the school curriculum, but when the government interprets literacy too narrowly it inadvertently impairs the educational foundation it intends to strengthen. It may very well limit the kinds of things everyone has a right to read.

The Department of Education must devote more time and resources to the problem of quality, especially in the secondary schools, than OE has done over the past fifteen years. A good starting point is the statement by Ernest Boyer, former Commissioner of Education: "It is quality which provides students the fundamental skills needed to function in our complicated world; which enables persons to fulfill themselves as individuals and effectively contribute to society" (Hearings Before a Subcommittee of the House Committee on Appropriations, 22 March 1979).

We would add particulars. First, regardless of their background, students are ill served if their education excludes the arts and humanities, which contribute in important ways to skills, personal fulfillment, and participation in the life of the community. Second, programs for disadvantaged students (notably under Title I) should not teach reading and writing simply as means for economic and social survival. It is fundamentally wrong to act as if access to the humanities were beyond the capabilities of such students; compensatory programs should demonstrate that, in the exercise of basic skills, students can discover, interpret, and enjoy many forms of human expression and freedom. Third, we recommend that Congress substantially increase the budget for Support and Innovation Grants under Title IV-C, which are administered by the states according to their own needs. Fourth, the National Institute of Education should apportion a larger share of its budget (which currently totals over $450 million) for research on how the humanities develop cognitive skills at various stages of learning and what makes some programs successful. Finally, *the Department of Education should define critical thinking as one of the basic skills that provides the foundation for advanced skills of all kinds.*

The National Endowment for the Humanities has supported the development of outstanding programs for the schools. Some of these, such as the National Humanities Faculty, involve collaboration between university faculty and schoolteachers in the development of curricula in the humanities. The NEH also funds the development of exemplary classroom materials and, since 1977, "extended teacher institutes" that integrate design of curriculum with new teaching techniques. Overall, however, the Endowment's approach to elementary and secondary education has been piecemeal and hesitant, partly because that portion of the agency's budget has always been small: it has remained at about $4.5 million in current dollars since FY1978, or 4.5 percent of the total definite program funds appropriated for FY1980. Since the Department of Education has primary federal reponsibility for the schools, NEH officials point out that they could not justify any significant increase in this figure before Congress. We are convinced that the urgency of the problem justifies doubling the budget for elementary and secondary education and maintaining appropriations at that percentage of program funds.

We think the NEH underestimates its power to improve the humanities in the schools. True, its funds are hardly equal to the enormous and complex task of strengthening the curriculum in thousands of school districts across the land. But the NEH has sponsored effective programs in the humanities for elementary and secondary students and can help fund new ones in the future. By publicizing exemplary programs more widely and by explaining the reasons for their success, the NEH can assist many schools to which it cannot offer direct program support. State Humanities Committees might help disseminate such information.

There is still another, relatively untried course of action entirely compatible with the charter and budget of the NEH. The Endowment's mission to promote public understanding of the humanities obligates the NEH to consider elementary and secondary education a significant public activity affecting the humanities. Exploring how a society educates its young and what a democracy demands from its schools is itself essential to the well-being of the humanities and American culture, and the Endowment should provide support for public discussion of these issues. Such a strategy will require some reallocation of funds in the Divisions of Public, State, and Special Programs, which serve chiefly—and perhaps too exclusively—the adult public. As part of their emphasis on the humanities and public policy, a few State Humanities Committees have supported programs on the schools, such as the 1977 forums presented in Georgia by the Atlanta Public Schools, the Ware County School System, and the Bacon County Board of Education. In every state, however, programs on elementary and secondary education constitute a tiny fraction of project grants—numbering, for example, 10 of 297 in Georgia from 1970 to 1977. For at least the next five years, the NEH's Divisions of Public, State, and Special Programs, with the cooperation of the State Humanities Committees and the Federation of Public Programs (a national federation of the State Committees), should sponsor forums and other projects on the humanities in elementary and secondary education and should identify this kind of activity as a priority in their program announcements.

Better means need to be found for coordinating the available resources of the NEH and the Department of Education. A possible model for cooperation, outlined in the recent Memorandum of Understanding by the Office of Education and the National Endowment for the Arts, expresses their common interests in arts education, the training of artists, and career development. Although this model may not be entirely appropriate for the NEH and the Department of Education, given the broader range of educational activities that they might share, greater interagency cooperation would give more visible assistance to states and local school districts. For example, the National Diffusion Network (NDN) helps school districts adopt programs approved by a panel of reviewers from the Office of Education and the National Institute of Education. Few of the programs disseminated through NDN, however, contribute directly to improving the humanities; programs developed with NEH support are rarely submitted to the review panel for evaluation. Working together, the two agencies should build a convincing case for requesting an increase of 25 percent in NDN's budget ($16 million proposed for FY1981) and for using the additional funds specifically for the dissemination of exemplary programs in the humanities and arts.

While we advocate better coordination between the two agencies, we must stress that their distinct missions require a continuation of *separate* federal administrations. In the NEH, the Division of Education Programs concentrates on the special characteristics of the humanities as disciplines for teaching and learning. It can view learning in the humanities as a continuous process spanning the primary grades, secondary and higher education, and adult or continuing education. Through the coordinated efforts of its several divisions, the NEH—unlike any other federal agency—can encourage collaboration among educational and cultural institutions and help develop links between humanistic scholarship and teaching.

In sum, we believe there has been a tendency for the NEH to

feel helpless about the schools' problems, and for OE to focus too narrowly on remedial education and the problems of the preliterate. Though the federal contribution makes up less than 10 percent of all funding for public education, the impact of federal programs at state and local levels far exceeds the dollars spent; particularly by disseminating information about successful educational practices, federal agencies can assist thousands of individual schools without intruding on local control of public education. Without slackening their resolve to make education a universal right, the federal agencies must help states and school districts revive the Jeffersonian ideal.

CURRICULUM: BEYOND THE BASICS

In American schools, the humanities are vulnerable not only to political and economic pressures, but also to unfortunate semantic and pedagogic distinctions. Most educators in the schools do not describe courses in reading, composition, literature, or history as "humanities" but as "language arts" or "social studies." Nor do they associate the humanities with critical thinking or the examination of values. They stamp the label *humanities* only on interdisciplinary courses in American and world culture or on the arts. We urge educators to view the humanities in terms of the links between skills, knowledge of cultural traditions, aesthetic judgment and enjoyment, and moral values. Teachers, librarians, administrators, and public officials must distance themselves from mercurial public moods, when necessary, and recall for everyone the broad educational goals of American schools.

RECOMMENDATION 4:   As an integral part of their commitment to quality in public and private education, local administrators should maintain in every elementary and secondary school a strong, well-structured curriculum in the humanities and arts. Continuously and step by step through the three major levels of learning, the curriculum ought to integrate training in expository, critical, and aesthetic skills with a firm factual base in cultural traditions.

Natural curiosity prompts children to raise questions about human existence; learning to read in the primary grades enables them to satisfy their curiosity independently. Joining the humanities to reading lessons at this level can show children some of the pleasures of discovery and expression—that there is joy in learning. Language skills must be the major objective of the curriculum in the early grades, but narrow utilitarian approaches to literacy can alienate children from the world of words just as it begins to reveal itself. In some reading programs, for example, students fill in worksheets and tests to advance from one instructional packet to the next. In many schools, writing lessons are utterly lifeless; they consist of short exercises in composition that require only a mechanical application of rules for placing words and sentences one after another. Several school districts in major regions of the United States use a computerized system for testing students' mastery of the increasingly difficult "concepts" found in what they study. Rarely under such circumstances do students have the chance to share discoveries with the teacher or with each other. Teachers often spend more time managing than teaching.

We do not quarrel with the view that learning must occur in a clearly articulated sequence or that students should acquire necessary skills before progressing to higher grades. Nor do we rule out the possibility that well-designed tests can serve this purpose. We would, however, reject any narrow interpretation of skills or overemphasis on testing that keeps children from learning to think.

In the primary grades, children should have direct experience of literature and the arts, to sharpen their senses and expand their ability to express themselves. Looking at art, playing and listening to music, dancing, reading poetry aloud, and enacting and retelling first-rate stories kindle group discussion and individual response. Indeed, the arts may be the best means for nurturing curiosity and creativity, and the best hope for identifying learning with enjoyment—in grade school and beyond.

• The humanities and arts intersect when children learn to describe their perceptions of art in words. The Aesthetic Education Program (developed by CEMREL, Inc., with support from the National Institute of Education) teaches a vocabulary for discussing art, music, dance, drama, and other art forms. One third grade teacher described how the unit "Constructing Dramatic Plot" carried over to other areas of the curriculum: after learning how the sequence of events creates dramatic interest in a play, students began to evaluate their reading textbooks, their own storytelling, and television programs according to how well plots were constructed (Stanley Madeja, *Through the Arts to the Aesthetic*, St. Louis, 1977).

At the upper elementary and middle school levels, the emphasis in the curriculum begins to shift from "learning to read" to "reading to learn." The interdependence of language and thinking, though axiomatic, is often ignored at this stage of learning. Here the humanities are indispensable for developing critical, conceptual, and imaginative skills and for introducing factual knowledge about cultural traditions. Thinking demands active synthesis of facts, not passive reception of them from images on a screen or words on a page. Thus reading, writing, and speaking must be integral parts of the curriculum at this level. Textbooks must interest and challenge students, not bore or coddle them—inferences, comparisons, and syntheses are as exciting to make as they are difficult.

Facts must be shown to have a living use, or they may deaden a young mind. In history and geography, for example, students should learn to visualize, classify, evaluate, and apply the facts at their command. The arts can give concrete form to the study of cultures, especially non-Western cultures and American subcultures with which students are unfamiliar. This calls for collaboration between school districts and museums, as in the East Cleveland Project of the Cleveland Museum of Art or in the New Orleans Museum of Art's program on Africa.

• Conceptual and critical skills can be taught through humanistic subjects not usually found at the middle school level, as in the Philosophy for Children program developed by Matthew Lipman, head of the Institute for the Advancement of Philosophy for Children at Montclair State College in New Jersey. This widely used program trains regular classroom instructors for teaching their students how to reflect systematically on thinking processes.

Without recourse to technical terms, students learn syllogistic reasoning, the difference between universal and particular statements, and other philosophical principles. These logical and analytical skills help children infer meaning from what they read. They begin to understand the importance of giving reasons for their views; out of this understanding, Lipman has observed, emerge an ability to think problems through and a dissatisfaction with glib opinions.

• In a number of schools, language and analytical skills are linked to cultural awareness through the study of Latin. The Language Transfer Project in Los Angeles, for example, trains regular classroom teachers to use Latin dialogues, readings, and songs that have been specially designed for developing students' linguistic and cultural awareness. Through Latin roots, students expand their English vocabulary and begin to recognize the relationship between Latin, English, and Spanish, the native language of many pupils in the district. One teacher in the program, which is based on similar projects in Philadelphia and Washington, D.C., noted a marked increase in her students' intellectual curiosity: when they encounter a new word, they reflect on its relationship to similar words. Children of various ethnic backgrounds and levels of ability seem equally enthusiastic about analyzing new words. Students also learn about mythology and other Roman cultural traditions.

At the secondary level, students should continue to develop their critical skills while learning how knowledge is organized in the disciplines of the humanities. In many secondary schools today writing assignments are few; they receive scant critical comment from teachers overloaded with large classes, bureaucratic paperwork, and committee assignments. The curriculum is fragmented, partly because government policy has encouraged a proliferation of subjects and has required schools to fulfill many specialized responsibilities. Arts education, when available at all, is generally separate from the regular curriculum, and many school libraries lack excellent media and print materials in the arts. Coherent interdisciplinary programs are rare. The humanistic disciplines must compete with each other and with other disciplines for meager resources. Students have to select from a smorgasbord of courses: the curriculum is linked neither horizontally nor vertically, often weighed down with a bewildering proliferation of electives. In short, many curricula fail to guide students from the fundamentals of learning to the foundations of knowledge.

The entire secondary school curriculum should emphasize the close relationship between writing and critical thinking, as advocated in the recent report of the Council for Basic Education's Commission on Writing (Clifton Fadiman and James Howard, *Empty Pages,* Belmont, Ca., 1979). Writing should engage a student with a subject worth writing about, not merely with the mechanics of spelling and grammar.

• In the Vermont Writing Program, based at the University of Vermont, teachers from around the state explore ways of revitalizing the teaching of composition in high schools. They improve their own writing as a first step toward understanding their students' writing problems. Based on the assumption that writing is more than a matter of rules laid down in textbooks, the program develops methods of teaching writing through literature, oral history, autobiography, and other humanistic subjects.

High schools should concentrate on an articulated sequence of courses in English, history, and foreign languages. Courses in these disciplines should not divorce skills and methods from knowledge of content and cultural context. English courses, which are currently some students' only contact with the humanities, should interweave composition and literature. Too often teachers trained in literature are bored by composition and neglect writing; conversely, teachers of composition frequently ignore the literary aspects of the subject. English courses need to emphasize the connections between expression, logic, and the critical use of textual and historical evidence.

Courses in history and social studies should deepen students' knowledge of the past and challenge them to compare the Western cultural heritage with those of other cultures. Courses in the social sciences such as psychology, sociology, or anthropology should not supplant the study of geography and history. No young person should be expected to understand the complex conceptual models used in the social sciences without first learning a solid base of factual knowledge and critical skills through the study of history. A promising recent development is the use of local historical resources in classes. Even more encouraging would be an increased use of the word *history* in the titles—and explicitly historical method in the content—of social studies courses.

Knowledge of foreign languages informs citizenship in the international community. Rather than being limited to the acquisition of basic language skills, the study of foreign language should aim toward more advanced linguistic skills and the cultural context of language. A greater emphasis on culture in foreign language study can deepen students' understanding of other cultures and develop an appreciation of the important contributions of linguistic minorities to our nation's culture. These minorities have long been ignored as a potential resource for enriching foreign language and cultural studies in the schools. In many schools, the coordination of language skills with knowledge of literature and culture is haphazard. The Modern Language Association's recent Task Forces recommended various steps for improving language study in American schools. We agree wholeheartedly with the Task Forces that foreign language study should increase students' "awareness of the nature and structure of language" and enlarge their understanding of foreign and American cultures (*Language Study for the 1980s: Reports of the MLA-ACLS Language Task Forces,* ed. Richard Brod, New York, 1980). The President's Commission on Foreign Language and International Studies reports that only 15 percent of all high school students now study a foreign language, compared with 24 percent in 1965; only 2 percent reach the third-year level. We share the Commission's concern about low enrollments, and we support its recommendation that colleges "reinvigorate language teaching in the schools" by raising the standards of their own requirements for admission (*Strength Through Wisdom,* Washington, D.C., 1979).

High school departments in the humanities should look to each other for common interests and comparative methods. Some programs integrate required courses in American history and literature. Others explore themes through literary classics and works of art from various cultures. Courses in single humanistic disciplines should use insights from the arts. Indeed, the appreciation of form and style is not confined to the arts; all teachers should explore the aesthetic dimensions of their subjects, or of allied fields—such as architecture—that cut across disciplines.

Courses in the humanities should probe connections between the humanities and other fields of knowledge. For example, humanistic questions are inherent in—and should foster an awareness of—the moral dimensions of science and technology. Teachers and students should consider the human purposes of scientific discovery and technological invention. The interconnections between the humanities and technology are especially important in regard to the new forms of communication transforming culture and our methods for understanding it—the electronic media and computers.

Especially for young people, television has become a natural source of information. It has given rise to new forms of entertainment and to new modes of learning that may complement or compete with learning in the schools. While preserving traditional methods, schools must recognize the new ones created by television. They must also cultivate what is sometimes called "media literacy"—a critical awareness of how television affects our thinking. Television's power to inform has profound civic, aesthetic, and cultural implications. Like a written text, the voice from the screen will not answer a direct question; no less than a written text, however, it must be regarded with critical vigilance. Though not yet so integral to our daily routines as television, computers will become increasingly important sources of information and tools for everyday living. They will influence our thinking and our expectations. So that young people can use informational technologies, the training of students in basic computer technology should begin in the schools. This training should aim beyond technical competence to an understanding of how such technologies affect our lives.

From kindergarten through twelfth grade, the humanities teach skills and subjects closely related to the civic purposes of education. Implicit in this educational process is a critical examination of human values. In today's parlance, however, the term *values education* has little to do with the humanities. Instead, it pertains to an array of educational practices—from programs emphasizing emotional development in personal relationships to attempts at improving school discipline.

As currently taught, some values education programs ignore broad historical and social contexts and focus instead on the process of making decisions. Through "sensitivity and sharing sessions," role playing, and other games, classes introduce students to dilemmas that result from the clash between different values. Students who act out conflicts may learn to understand themselves better; they may also learn to tolerate views other than their own. Conducted superficially or taken to extremes, however, this approach to values may teach only the false virtue of polite acquiescence—how to sidestep rather than confront thorny questions. If too much emphasis is put on tolerating all points of view and on problem solving in simulated "experience," students may not learn the civic virtue of acting responsibly and with conviction in real life.

Making responsible judgments requires well-developed critical and imaginative abilities. Students can learn values indirectly, by reflecting on the actions of others and drawing from value-laden examples. For learning about values, whether the goal is civic responsibility or personal moral growth, few strategies can rival the time-honored practice of identifying with characters in literature and history who, caught in ethical dilemmas, have had to make a choice. We would not, however, limit the discussion of values to courses in the humanities or in citizenship. Questions about values should arise throughout the curriculum, notably in the sciences and social sciences. In science courses students should be introduced to the moral responsibilities of scientists and technicians, past and present.

• The program Law in a Free Society, based in Santa Monica, California, explores the ethical dimensions of current legal and political problems. Teachers read political and legal philosophy as background for their classroom discussions on authority, property, and justice. Students study court cases, selections from works of literature, and accounts of historical incidents.

• In a physics course developed in Vergennes, Vermont,

students consider questions arising from the convergence of science and the humanities. For example, the scientific concepts needed to understand Galileo's discoveries are taught along with some of the human implications of those discoveries—Galileo's personal dilemma and the philosophical and religious controversy of the period.

The texts of the humanities offer examples of human moral response that should be analyzed critically as possible models for action. Students must be encouraged to look to the past not for dogmatic answers but for perspective.

TEACHING

The low status of the teaching profession is a national disgrace and an obstacle to improving education in the schools. Teachers of the humanities in particular are often held in low esteem. To many people the teaching of English or history does not appear to demand the special expertise required for chemistry or mathematics. Underscoring this regrettable attitude, some tenured teachers who survive dismissals following drops in enrollments are reassigned to teach humanistic subjects outside their major area of training and experience.

We cannot ask teachers in the humanities to mediate sensitively between students' lives and the world of ideas and values unless we improve the day-to-day atmosphere in which they work. Too often, paperwork and custodial duties take so much of a teacher's time and energy as to leave little for teaching, much less for reading or reflection. Each day, high school teachers typically teach five or six classes; each class is commonly filled with thirty or more students of widely varying abilities. Heavy teaching loads make individual instruction virtually impossible. "Life in the trenches"—not an inaccurate metaphor for teaching in many schools—has forced many able teachers to retire early or seek another career.

RECOMMENDATION 5:   School boards and superintendents should reduce classes to manageable size. Classes in writing should be limited to twenty students.

Hard work discourages most teachers only when it does not produce results in the classroom; the satisfaction of seeing students progress is an incentive for good teaching. How can more teachers enjoy that satisfaction? As one step, school boards and superintendents should keep class size within reasonable limits. Reduction from thirty to twenty students or fewer usually improves student achievement. In composition classes, twenty should be the maximum. Larger classes lower a teacher's incentive to assign meaningful amounts of written work and prevent conscientious response to each student's writing problems. Class size can be reduced if school boards and superintendents will give imaginative attention to scheduling and refresh their sense of priorities: capable teachers are more valuable in class than in support or supervisory positions.

Further pedagogic advantages can result from new instructional technologies. Even when used in the classroom with maximum effectiveness, computer-aided instruction (CAI) and tutored video instruction (TVI) do not replace a teacher. Either or both, however, can free some of a teacher's time for substantive criticism of a student's work and give a student more opportunities for independent study. Of these two technologies, CAI seems particularly useful in teaching foreign languages and the technical aspects of writing. We recognize that many technologies are costly, that their quality and reliability must be proven in every case, and that teachers who view technology with suspicion are not necessarily Luddites. We advocate intelligent, discriminating application of electronic technologies in the classroom as their capabilities increase and their costs decline.

RECOMMENDATION 6: To provide teachers with a full range of opportunities for their professional development, state and federal agencies as well as private foundations should increase support for programs that enable teachers to study, travel, and participate in professional activities. School boards should provide released time and incentives for teachers to take advantage of available programs for their own intellectual renewal.

Many programs in staff development emphasize classroom

management, techniques for improving teaching effectiveness, or the use of new curricular materials. These can be useful, but neither they nor small classes meet all the needs of teachers. Teachers must also have opportunity and stimulus for intellectual renewal and enrichment. When school boards shun workshops or summer institutes, or when teachers fail to take advantage of the discretionary time written into their union contracts to advance their knowledge of their subjects, they reject invaluable means of revitalizing classrooms. Both attitudes are particularly damaging when, because of declining school enrollments, school districts can hire few new teachers and are thus virtually cut off from a major source of new ideas and enthusiasm.

Sabbaticals and other special programs are a privilege. Selection should recognize and stimulate excellence in teaching. This kind of reward is especially encouraging to teachers because they seldom receive salary increases for teaching well. Because of the virtual disappearance of paid sabbaticals from the budgets of school districts, state, federal, and private sources of funds are a necessity. We urge that they help teachers pursue academic study rather than advanced degrees in educational administration or counseling, which often lure good teachers out of the classroom forever.

Sabbaticals and summer institutes have more than an immediate effect on teaching performance. They can inspire teachers for the rest of their careers. A number of teachers who participated in the National Defense Education Act summer institutes and the John Hay Fellows program in the 1960s remember these experiences as a high point in their professional development, an encouragement to continue to teach well, and a source of long professional relationships. Teachers who have received national recognition report that they have more influence on school policies in general: for example, a teacher designated by the National Humanities Faculty as a "Master Teacher" has noticed that fellow teachers now seek out her opinion on questions of curriculum and that supervisors respect her views on district-wide programs.

Before this recommendation is dismissed as unrealistic in a time of fiscal constraint, all who share responsibility for our schools should reflect on this: what we seek to advance is nothing less than the quality of the educational experience of our young. Unless the intellectual vitality of the educational system is restored from top to bottom, no number of bureaucratic or technological or economic achievements will mean much to the future of our society.

RECOMMENDATION 7:   We recommend that learned societies take a more active interest in the education and professional development of high school teachers in the humanities. Learned societies should develop guidelines for the education of teachers in humanistic disciplines and sponsor workshops and conferences to help teachers further their knowledge.

The American Historical Association (AHA), the Modern Language Association, and the American Philosophical Association have begun to pay attention to the needs of high school teachers. The associations have encountered problems, the largest of which is the gap between those who write about their fields and those who teach but do not publish. Many publishing scholars have little regard for high school teachers. Program sessions on scholarship and teaching at the AHA's national convention serve two distinct clienteles, and the AHA's effort to designate exemplary high school history teachers has had mixed success. The association's most successful attempt to bring teachers and scholars together has been joint conferences on specific topics in the teaching of history. Stimulated by new ideas, teachers return from these meetings with a heightened sense of their importance in the larger scheme of the academic profession. Learned societies themselves can learn from this experience and expand on it. It is not only schoolteachers who suffer from the artificial barriers between secondary and post-secondary education. In the long run the national repute of the learned societies and the health of their disciplines in higher education depend in some measure on high school teachers in the humanities.

RECOMMENDATION 8:   We urge state departments of education—whatever use they make of competency tests—to base requirements for certification of teachers on a solid liberal education that includes the humanities. While we recognize the need for assuring the competency of teachers, we fear that minimum competency requirements for certification may become maximum standards.

Selectivity is badly needed in the education and certification of teachers. The blunt data show that students in the field of education are typically among the least academically proficient undergraduates. Information from the American College Testing Program for 1975–76, for example, indicates that in a sample of freshmen from nineteen fields, education majors ranked fourteenth in English and seventeenth in math. In the National Longitudinal Study sample, college seniors of 1976 with a major in education ranked fourteenth out of sixteen fields on Scholastic Aptitude Test (SAT) verbal scores and fifteenth of the sixteen fields in math (W. Timothy Weaver, "In Search of Quality: The Need for Talent in Teaching," *Phi Delta Kappan*, September 1979). Traditional procedures for certification, requiring a candidate to complete an accredited college program, have not kept incompetent teachers out of the classroom. As a result, many states have established competency-based requirements. Many have also increased the number of education courses required for certification.

We are skeptical of these new trends in the selection of teachers. Competency testing is based on the assumption that minimum skills for adequate teaching can be defined and measured; it does not reward achievement beyond a minimum standard. Education courses crowd substantive liberal arts courses out of a student's program. In Massachusetts, for example, it is now almost impossible for a student to complete both liberal arts degree requirements and education requirements in a normal four-year program. The increasing number of requirements for certification imposed by the state of Oregon has led Reed College, a private liberal arts institution, to drop its Master of Arts in Teaching program. Something is radically wrong with our system of certifying teachers when it virtually excludes people with Ph.D.'s in academic fields and forces prospective teachers, in their undergraduate years, to reduce the number of courses they take in the disciplines they will be teaching.

The content of education for teachers is far more important than the attainment of narrow, measurable objectives. All teachers need a solid general education based on the humanities, sciences, and social sciences, to which they can add courses on—and practical experience in—how to teach. Suggestions for improving the preparation of teachers should come from joint discussions—for which administrative support will be necessary—between college faculty in the arts and sciences and faculty in schools of education, and from successful classroom teachers. Learned societies should develop recommendations for the training of teachers in the humanities, as the National Council for Accreditation of Teacher Education has suggested to us. If states continue to increase the number of required courses in education, then perhaps the training of teachers should extend beyond four years to insure a solid academic background. At both public and private institutions, five-year programs—a four-year B.A. program, with a major in an academic field, and a year of additional courses in education—may provide the best foundation.

For a long time women have been the major source of personnel for the teaching profession. Now the women's movement and affirmative action have encouraged them to choose other careers, reducing the pool of talented candidates for vacant positions in the nation's classrooms. The number of such positions has diminished, but the importance of their being filled by outstanding teachers has never been greater. Schools of education cannot meet this need by lowering their academic standards in order to attract students and keep their programs alive. Liberal arts faculty also have an important obligation. Some professors dissuade bright young people from going into teaching, or denigrate the career so that anyone entering it feels inferior. If college humanists are to help prepare good schoolteachers, they must show genuine respect for the teaching profession.

SCHOOL-COLLEGE COLLABORATION

Collaboration between schools and colleges is a most important strategy for strengthening the humanities in the schools. In 1973 the Carnegie Commission on Higher Education noted two persistent obstacles to collaboration: differences in attitude and social status between school and college teachers; and political difficulties arising from separate bureaucratic jurisdictions over elementary-secondary and higher education (*Continuity and Discontinuity: Higher Education and the Schools*, New York). Since 1973 a number of programs have begun to surmount the first of these obstacles. The second is still formidable. The success of collaboration depends not only on the goodwill of interested teachers, but also on the long-term commitment of educational institutions. Administrations, with added support from public and private agencies, must actively promote joint discussion of vital issues in curriculum and instruction.

RECOMMENDATION 9:   We recommend that colleges and universities encourage their faculty to help improve education in the humanities in high schools.

Responsibility for coordinating high school and college curricula rests ultimately with administrators at both levels. Schools must give teachers released time for participating in professional activities relating to the curriculum. Colleges and universities must recognize faculty service to elementary and secondary education through their systems of academic incentives and rewards.

Deficiencies in learning hamper the high school student who goes on to college, especially in foreign languages and writing, which demand constant practice and a sequential development of skills. At the other extreme, unnecessary duplication of the high school curriculum in college leads to boredom and waste. More coordination between schools and colleges would help insure that education proceeds productively from one stage to the next. As one way of taking more interest in the schools, learned societies should sponsor activities that will strengthen the continuity of learning in the humanities between high school and college. Reliable mechanisms for cooperative monitoring of the curriculum are particularly important for high schools and local community colleges with open admissions. At the same time, college and university faculty should help schools plan the education of those students (about 50 percent) who will not go on to higher education; young people must not be deprived of learning in the humanities just because their formal education terminates with the twelfth grade.

• The Advanced Placement (A.P.) Program of the College Board may serve as a general model for improving high school courses while linking them to the college curriculum. Each A.P. course is the responsibility of a development committee made up of secondary school and college teachers appointed by the College Board. The committee discusses teaching methods, course content, and instructional materials; the College Board publishes an annual description of each course. Although the program serves only a fraction of the high school population, its impact on participating institutions goes beyond the students enrolled in A.P. courses. The teachers in the program exchange information on the state of their disciplines and convey what they have learned to colleagues.

Many colleges and universities can directly influence the content of the high school curriculum through their requirements for admission. We recognize the diversity of institutions and their widely different policies. All institutions, however, have an obligation to help high schools prepare students to meet current requirements: first, by expressing their expectations clearly to the schools; and second, by encouraging faculty to work with the schools.

• The new entrance assessment in writing at the University of Michigan exemplifies an admissions policy designed to improve the quality of students' high school preparation. As part of a university-wide program for improving undergraduate writing under the direction of the English Composition Board (ECB), the policy helps insure continuity between high school and college writing programs. High schools seek the services of the ECB to insure that their students will meet the new standards. The ECB instructs high school teachers in specific teaching methods that have been developed at the university and shows the relationship between high school composition and the university writing program. Teachers hope that the university will help convince school administrators to reduce teaching loads for more effective writing instruction.

Methods similar to Michigan's might be used by other institutions—for English and other humanistic subjects, notably foreign languages. Colleges and universities should regard their obligation to help high schools not as a drain upon resources but as an investment in the future of higher education.

RECOMMENDATION 10:   Because schools change slowly, we endorse models of school-college collaboration that emphasize long-term cooperation. We recommend that more colleges or universities and school districts adopt such programs for their mutual benefit, and that funding sources sustain programs and administrative costs on a continuing basis.

Programs of school-college collaboration offer the best opportunity to strengthen instruction in the schools while providing intellectual renewal for teachers. Not all models of collaboration are equally effective. Programs that bring teachers together for a workshop with no follow-up have a major drawback: many participants cannot keep up their enthusiasm alone once they return to their schools. The best models involve teams of teachers and administrators from participating schools and meet two prerequisites for implementing change in the schools: teacher "ownership" of the program and strong administrative support (Paul Berman and Milbrey W. McLaughlin, *Federal Programs Supporting Educational Change*, Vol. 8: *Implementing and Sustaining Innovations*, Santa Monica, Ca., 1978).

Long-range improvement ultimately depends on long-term support. Ideally, collaboration should be a local concern, with school districts and colleges or universities in close proximity working together to assure high quality. They should share costs as well as administrative and program responsibilities for periods of five years or more. School districts without a nearby college or university should be able to find assistance elsewhere from faculty in higher education, with support from public and private sources.

• Some universities and schools have developed collaborative programs to train high school teachers in teaching composition. One of the oldest and most influential of these is the Bay Area Writing Project. Since its modest beginnings at the University of California at Berkeley in 1974, the program has expanded nationally with NEH support to fifty-six sites, each of which serves a limited geographic region and draws upon the resources of a local university. The project selects outstanding school and college composition teachers to attend summer institutes. Although experts in the field of educational research address the group, they do not dictate teaching methods. After the summer institute, teachers serve as writing consultants in their own schools and continue to exchange information about successful teaching practices throughout the school year. In the belief that writing skills should not be the sole responsibility of English teachers, the project trains teachers from all subject areas.

• The Yale-New Haven Teacher Institute provides a promising model of collaboration between a major university and a local school district. It integrates curricular development in the humanities with intellectual renewal for teachers, stressing a collegial relationship between Yale faculty and New Haven teachers. Since 1970 the university and the school district have jointly developed curricular units in history; the Teacher Institute extends this cooperative relationship to other subjects in the humanities. Teachers plan units reflecting the insights gained through independent study and seminar discussions guided by Yale faculty.

• Another model of collaboration involves higher education faculty selected from across the country by the National Humanities Faculty (NHF) for their abilities to work well with high school teachers. The NHF's current Program for the Development of Humanities Disciplines Within the Schools draws from ten years' experience in bringing college and university humanists into schools. In this program, currently reaching twenty-six schools, visiting humanists observe and teach classes. They also advise a core team of teachers and administrators about ways to revitalize courses in the humanities. Contact between school and college faculty extends over an eighteen-month period, with seventeen days of faculty advisors' visits spread through the school year and a two-week summer institute.

• A variation on the NHF model is the pilot Humanists-in-the-Schools program currently sponsored by the California Council for the Humanities. It brings younger humanists—graduate students or recent Ph.D.'s—from the University of California at Berkeley into schools in the nearby San Mateo School District for a three-month assignment. Teachers and students seem to view the visiting humanists as a valuable resource.

The impact of collaborative programs cannot be measured simply by the numbers of schools served, although this too is impressive. Schools involved in such programs generally report a resurgence of interest in the humanities among faculty, students, and, in some cases, the surrounding community. The models cited above have made considerable progress in improving the humanities in the schools. They and new models like them need help to survive long enough to lead to significant improvement. Such projects rely to a great extent on support from the NEH or private foundations. These sources willingly fund programs but rarely administrative costs, especially if they are likely to be long-term. Grantors must help relieve applicants of annual and time-consuming paperwork. Sources of support should not abandon demonstrably successful programs in search of new ideas. They should provide long-term support for the administrative costs required to bring schools and colleges together with lasting effect. Finally, we reiterate the need for the new Department of Education and the NEH to make exemplary programs widely known.

Our conception of good elementary and secondary education is both progressive and conservative. None of the institutions that share the task of educating our young people can afford to look only to the past. By its very nature education looks toward the future, and our nation's schools have always been sustained by a powerful dream of the future—that a life of decency and dignity, enriched by learning, is open to all. Our recommendations also draw strength from the ideals of the past that the humanities transmit. Our children must not be denied this source of strength, for they face a future in which revolutionary changes—already foreshadowed by today's technology—will demand old and new capacities for thought and communication. As the first generation that truly deserves the sobriquet "children of the media," young people today are largely detached from the literary and historical bases of culture that previous generations took for granted. They therefore need, probably more than any generation before them, eloquent evidence of the duration of human culture and reassurance that they are a living part of that culture.

CHAPTER THREE 🌿

The Humanities
and Higher Education

Like a Janus with two unhappy faces, higher education in the United States gazes upon a tumultuous recent past and an uncertain future. Emerging from a period of extraordinary growth, during which they extended access to new students and performed new services for society, our colleges and universities are implicated more deeply than ever before in our national life. They contribute immeasurably to material progress and public discourse as well as to education, and they are scrutinized as never before. The campus turmoil of the late 1960s has abated, but so has the boom in higher education. The prospects now include little or no growth in enrollments, financial difficulties, complex relationships with government and the public, and conflicting demands from a society itself riven with uncertainties.

How higher education responds to the many claims upon it during the next two decades will be a crucial chapter in the history of our culture. Whatever the response, we know that it cannot depend on major increases in financial support. We take this harsh fact into account as much as possible. Such constraints give even greater urgency to the task of revitalizing the services that higher education and the humanities render each other.

One great strength of American higher education, both public and private, is its diversity. This and the autonomy of individual institutions are to be cherished, but they give no license for the incoherence that is for some institutions among the legacies of change. Colleges and universities must manage limited resources prudently and see their social missions clearly. They must also reconsider their educational ideals and translate them into coherent, purposeful academic programs. The humanities, concerned with what human beings know and how they use their knowledge, can share in no more fitting task than this rethinking.

At many institutions liberal or general education, which for several generations guaranteed a presence for the humanities in every undergraduate's course of study, has so declined that the Carnegie Foundation for the Advancement of Teaching has called it "a disaster area" (*Missions of the College Curriculum,* San Francisco, 1977). Faced with an uncertain economy and job market, a disorderly curriculum, and educators' diminished confidence in the purpose of a college education, many undergraduates choose majors narrowly aimed at obtaining a first job. They seem unaware that most subjects, disciplines, and careers intersect the humanities. Humanists themselves often neglect the connections between their disciplines and education in the natural and social sciences, engineering, business, and other fields. Laden with narrowly conceived courses and lacking clear progression through the disciplines, the curriculum in the humanities at some institutions has become so overspecialized that it merely prepares for graduate study in the humanities rather than contributes to a liberal education. Students confront a welter of courses that bear little relation to each other, to other disciplines, or to their own interests. Finally, the college curriculum has yet to find a satisfactory accommodation between the idea of a common cultural tradition and the legitimate claims of racial and ethnic cultures to their own traditions in the humanities.

The diminishing of the humanities is only one aspect of a disarray in liberal education whose consequence is well known: college students whose education leaves them uneducated. Many have no command of written and spoken English. Without well-developed skills in foreign languages, most lack the valuable understanding of other cultures that grows from such skills. Many scarcely know their own culture—its history, literature, art, and thought—and how it shapes their lives.

Schools and departments of graduate education for the professions are paying more attention to questions of value, choice, and responsibility that often link their fields to the humanities. Yet many students, responding to the admissions policies of professional schools, seek little exposure to the humanities during their undergraduate years and are ill equipped for examining the humanistic dimensions of their professional training. Faculty in the humanities show little willingness, often less than their colleagues in the professional schools, to explore these dimensions.

Graduate education in the humanities is in a state of uncertainty. As undergraduate enrollments and faculty expansion have subsided, new and mid-career Ph.D.'s in the humanities have found fewer and fewer positions as teachers and scholars. The plight of these people is a pressing concern. So is the need to insure the continuity of humanistic scholarship by attracting the best talent to graduate training of the highest quality. Graduate programs must adapt to a smaller academic job market. They must also help return the humanities to the mainstream of undergraduate education: to demonstrate anew the importance of the humanities in liberal education, higher education will need generalists as well as specialists in the humanities.

Our colleges and universities have helped make American humanistic scholarship competitive with the finest in the world, but support for advanced research in the humanities is insecure. Rising costs threaten sabbaticals and library resources. Declining government support for science may leave institutions less able to fund the humanities. Inflation also diminishes the purchasing power of funds from private foundations, corporations, and government agencies.

The diversity of American colleges and universities allows no single agenda for strengthening the humanities. In recent years many institutions have begun to reassess their aims, often with a view to strengthening the humanities in the regular curriculum and in adult or continuing education. Here and in the next chapter we cite ways the humanities might best serve, and be served by, our colleges. We are aware that what works for one institution will not necessarily work for others. We offer proposals flexible enough to help many kinds of institutions, but we emphasize that the humanities must be a part of all public and private higher education. Because the humanities ask what it means to be human, their importance to higher education is self-evident: in work or leisure, parenthood or friendship, citizenship or solitude, our college and university graduates should be sensitive to the moral, spiritual, and cultural life of the community. The methods common to the humanities enable educated people to share their experience and define its quality.

UNDERGRADUATE EDUCATION

To claim that the humanities today form the core of a college education would sound a hollow cry. When the Commission on the Humanities of 1964 associated the humanities with a program of education "based on the liberal tradition we inherit from classical antiquity," it rightly invoked an enduring connection that once unified the curriculum by virtually identifying the humanities with the liberal arts. But the growth of knowledge and the multiplication of educational missions over the past century have repeatedly challenged this liberal tradition of learning and thus the humanities' place in the curriculum.

Until well into the nineteenth century, the humanities dominated an undergraduate curriculum whose vocational, educational, and social purposes were in harmony. The early American college had three basic aims: to train young men for the clergy or political leadership; to develop the mental discipline and moral and religious habits appropriate to a cultivated gentleman, whatever his vocation; and to maintain, through induction into the traditions of classical culture, a small elite of the educated in a predominantly agricultural society. These goals, educators thought, could be achieved through studies in the literature, history, and culture of Western antiquity, combined with religious instruction. Through the humanities the early college expressed its faith in the coherence of knowledge, in a single cultural tradition, and in the community of the learned.

Revolutionary intellectual and social changes weakened that

faith. The explosion of knowledge in the second half of the nineteenth century scattered the fields of academic inquiry beyond the reach of a single curriculum or small faculty. To impose order on this fragmentation, newborn universities divided into schools, departments, disciplines, and specialties. Universities also took on a new responsibility for higher education: research, the pursuit of new knowledge for its own sake and for the benefit of society. The sciences gained a prominence in the universities that has never since been challenged. Humanistic learning also profited from the new emphasis on research, but in the curriculum the division and subdivision of knowledge eroded common ground formerly occupied by the humanities.

Founded as institutions where, in the words of Ezra Cornell, "any person can find instruction in any study," the new universities also expanded the social mission of higher education. They did not educate an elite as socially exclusive or all-male as the earlier colleges had. Studies preparing students for skilled occupations, formerly relegated to apprenticeships, found their way into the curriculum, especially at the comprehensive land grant institutions established by the Morrill Act of 1862. Vocational training in college education attracted new students and taught new technologies required by a society growing rapidly in population and industry.

As new arts and sciences arose and utility rivaled cultivation, liberal education was redefined as a synthesis of new studies and old ideals. The curriculum became a catalog—much as we know it today—of branches of knowledge and kinds of expertise needed by society. Colleges and universities entered the twentieth century offering an emporium of courses in place of the old curriculum of humane studies. Organization of the undergraduate course of study into the major and electives reflected the increasingly specialized character of knowledge and gave students freedom to follow their own interests. Undergraduate education was called liberal insofar as institutions required students to take survey courses in the major fields of knowledge and satisfy distribution requirements.

The humanities remained an essential part of liberal learning through the first half of this century. They claimed far less of the curriculum than previously, but institutions still looked to them to fulfill inherited ideals of liberal education. One of these was civic: the humanities helped prepare students for responsible participation in society. A second ideal was personal: the humanities offered spiritual and emotional enrichment. Liberal education, which became widely known as general education, usually included requirements in the humanities. Through survey courses in Western culture, for example, many institutions expected generations of students to shape their civic and personal values. Surveys of the Western tradition also provided a common educational experience—another traditional ideal of liberal education—for an increasingly diversified student body.

The synthesis of modern curriculum and older educational ideals, never an entirely stable one, has disintegrated since the Second World War. The steady extension of educational opportunity—first under the G.I. Bill and later through civil rights reforms, affirmative action, and the growth of community colleges—challenged the notions of a common culture and an even partially unified curriculum. Disturbed by our nation's policies at home and abroad and suspecting higher education of complicity in them, students in the 1960s rejected the idea that educational institutions inculcated civic virtue or offered personal enrichment. The idea of a central Western cultural tradition came under attack as elitist and irrelevant. Many institutions granted students greater freedom in their course of study. Distribution requirements were cut back, required courses in the humanities often abandoned, the ideal of a common educational experience lost.

After a century of readjustment and some years of disintegration, liberal education and the humanities were especially vulnerable to the wave of vocationalism that swept undergraduate learning in the 1970s. Students saw that they would have to compete with millions of other college graduates for employment in an uncertain economy. They looked to their undergraduate years not for breadth, civic ideals, or personal enrichment, but for the skills that would get them a job. Nationwide between 1969 and 1976 the number of preprofessional majors grew dramatically.

This growth coincided with a reduction of general education or breadth requirements from 43 percent to 34 percent of the typical course of study. Majors and total enrollments in the humanities declined *(Missions of the College Curriculum)*. Some of our more than three thousand colleges and universities were able to maintain a firm commitment to liberal education; yet no type of institution proved immune to vocationalism. Indeed, some traditional liberal arts colleges, facing financial hardship and falling enrollments, shifted their focus to career education.

At all kinds of institutions, faculty and administrators withdrew from the business of shaping a coherent philosophy of education. Free to choose, students chose vocationalism. Liberal education and the humanities, their fates still linked, were willed to the periphery of undergraduate learning.

As higher education enters the 1980s, it must formulate afresh the ideals of liberal education. New models of a liberal curriculum must accommodate the various backgrounds and goals of today's students, including their concern with careers. Liberal education has in fact always served career needs. As Alfred North Whitehead said:

> The antithesis between a technical and liberal education is fallacious. There can be no adequate technical education which is not liberal, and no liberal education which is not technical: that is, no education which does not impart both technique and intellectual vision. (*The Aims of Education and Other Essays,* New York, 1929)

The humanities—without excluding other kinds of learning— are essential for intellectual vision. Properly conceived, liberal education includes the humanities along with the other major fields of knowledge. But liberal education must aim beyond breadth; it must search for the connections among fields of knowledge and between knowledge and its uses. As the home of philosophy, history, and criticism, the humanities guide that search and thus have a special place in liberal education.

Every institution of higher learning must affirm the importance of the humanities. In the highly specialized circumstances of military education, for example, the humanities should be considered necessary for training responsible leaders; we have been struck with the fact that, in letters to us, the commanders of several military academies have stressed that the humanities help develop the ability to reason and communicate and that they confer an understanding of the social and ethical dimensions of military policy. A fundamentally different kind of institution, the private liberal arts college, has traditionally honored the humanities as central to the curriculum; colleges with religious affiliations have long upheld the humanities as essential for religious education. Yet even these customary homes of liberal learning will have to revivify the humanities for students ignorant of the cultural and social values of past generations.

In general, it may be that the more dependent an institution is on public funding and the more vocational its charter, the more broadly administrators and faculty should construe the idea of brokerage between the humanities and the career interests of students. Liberal studies such as the humanities must often justify their importance alongside the technical and vocational missions of state colleges and universities, land grant institutions, community colleges, and technical institutes. These institutions may find it particularly fruitful to draw students toward study of the humanities through programs that integrate the humanities with career preparation.

Community colleges have become leaders of the movement to provide greater equality of opportunity in higher education. With over four million students, these institutions now account for over one-third of all enrollments in higher education. Career and technical education are among the most important services provided by community colleges. But the notion that community colleges need not provide all students a general education—a view shared by some state legislatures and regulatory agencies, many students, and indeed some community college administrators—is mistaken. Two recent conferences on the humanities in two-year institutions issued far-reaching recommendations for strengthening the humanities; both conferences emphasized the need for curricula integrating the humanities with occupational education (*Challenges Before the Humanities in Community Colleges,* ed.

Donald D. Schmeltekopf and Anne D. Rassweiler, Cranford, N.J., 1980; and *Strengthening Humanities in Community Colleges,* ed. Roger Yarrington, Washington, D.C., 1980).

In times of tight budgets, colleges and universities of all kinds will find it difficult to add new programs in the humanities. As the Committee on the Humanities of the American Association of State Colleges and Universities (AASCU) reported to us, "Given the difficulty of maintaining existing programs, administrators and faculty regard the development of new programs as impossible. Ironically, the ability to initiate change may now be particularly critical to the humanities." Educators will have to make some hard choices. Humanities departments, the Council of Graduate Schools has said to us, should

> consider whether, as is typical, the largest portion of their course offerings should be directed to departmental majors. Offerings for the major should, perhaps, be reduced and even then be more varied, so as to be only one strand of a department's offerings, while new courses of interest and service to students in other preparations should be developed.

Reasserting the humanities' central place in liberal education depends on connecting them with other fields of study without abandoning the valuable contribution of traditional, discipline-centered courses in the humanities. As the AASCU Committee concluded,

> Often movement toward change is seen as an erosion of the strength of traditional programs. The real challenge is to discover ways of maintaining the balance between meeting changing student needs and identifying new roles for the humanities *and* maintaining the strength of the humanities disciplines.

Underlying our recommendations on undergraduate and professional education is a belief that the humanities develop capacities and perspectives necessary for every individual: they are essential in careers over a lifetime; they are essential beyond careers. The first of these ideas is one that students and administrators—and indeed humanists—need to be reminded of today. The second idea liberal education has kept alive always.

RECOMMENDATION 11: Efforts to give fresh meaning to liberal education must continue; all such efforts should emphasize the importance of the humanities for developing the mental capacities and historical knowledge needed for
- —effective command of written and spoken English;
- —enjoyment and informed judgment of the arts;
- —understanding (preferably based on knowledge of foreign languages) of other cultures;
- —analysis and assessment of ethical problems, issues of public policy, and the questions of value underlying science and technology.

Rooted in language and dependent in particular on writing, the humanities are inescapably bound to literacy. From reading works of literature, history, and philosophy, or the symbolic texts of music and the visual arts, humanists proceed to elaborate their insights through language. Traditionally the humanities, especially departments of English, have trained undergraduates in the use of language. Yet the effective use of English does not end with the humanities or with formal education. To read and listen for comprehension; to have a feeling for the complexity of discourse; to speak and write clearly and persuasively: these are useful in every area of learning, working, and living.

In literature and the arts, acts of the imagination give public expression to private experience. Liberal education should develop the senses for appreciating form and beauty. Literature, painting, music, dance, and other art forms have intimate connections with ideas. Thus the fullest response to art depends on knowledge of the history and characteristics of the artist's chosen medium, and on an understanding of the interplay of individual talent, aesthetics, artistic tradition, and historical context. Study of the humanities fosters this knowledge and understanding.

The humanities have always been associated with the civic purpose of liberal education—to prepare the individual for making informed choices and acting responsibly. This purpose must be reasserted today, with a special urgency. As instant communications deluge us with information on social and political issues, we face civic choices more complex and perhaps more numerous than ever before. The humanities emphasize interpretation and criticism, indispensable techniques for participating in community life and keeping watch over its values. Each major branch of the humanities helps educate men and women for citizenship. History provides clues for understanding the present. Literature broadens personal moral vision through exploring character, circumstance, and choice. Philosophy supplies rules of analysis and criteria for belief.

Today the responsible citizen must look beyond native borders. The political, economic, and cultural interdependence of nations affects our everyday lives and will shape our common future. Under these circumstances, the dwindling of foreign language and international studies in American higher education represents a dangerous parochialism. Knowledge of a foreign language improves comprehension of one's own language and of foreign culture. Knowledge of geography and the history of other societies illuminates one's own culture and the complexity of culture in general.

In 1966, according to the President's Commission on Foreign Language and International Studies, one-third of American colleges and universities required knowledge of a foreign language for admission; only 8 percent do now. The percentage of undergraduates enrolling in international studies is now barely half of what it was a decade ago (*Strength Through Wisdom*, Washington, D.C., 1979). We concur with the President's Commission: liberal education must renew its commitment to foreign language and international studies by strengthening foreign language requirements, expanding programs in area studies, and teaching more courses in the regular curriculum from an international perspective. (Similar concerns guide the Council on Learning's current project, Education and the World View, which will assess college students' understanding of global perspectives and identify needs in international education.)

A more than passing acquaintance with the natural and social sciences is inseparable from the critical and interpretive capacities developed through the humanities. Science and technology transform the conditions of life in beneficial ways. They also raise serious moral and civic questions: genetic engineering; the chemical control of human behavior and reproduction; euthanasia; the distribution of space, fuel, and other diminishing natural resources; the electronic invasion of privacy; and so forth. The social sciences—psychology, sociology, anthropology, economics, and political science—furnish insights into the organization of human societies, and these interpretations influence public policies as well as the day-to-day behavior of individuals. The humanities offer historical perspective and critical methods necessary for discussing the problems presented by other disciplines. If the aim is to make invention creative and humane, knowledge of the humanities must be coupled with an understanding of the characteristics of scientific inquiry and technological change.

Liberal education must define scientific literacy as no less important a characteristic of the educated person than reading and writing. As an especially important part of this literacy, students must learn about new informational technologies, which affect society today as significantly as did printing centuries ago and television during the last thirty years. At present no more than 40 percent of American college students graduate with some basic knowledge of how to use a computer. Computer literacy must now be considered among the goals of a liberal education by all colleges and universities; the training of undergraduates in the use of computers should include consideration of the social repercussions of informational technologies.

Liberal education must find an effective compromise between the individual's choice among many courses and the institution's responsibility to provide a coherent educational experience. Faculty from all disciplines must sacrifice personal and parochial interests if these work against a new synthesis of curriculum and ideals.

RECOMMENDATION 12: While no single curriculum is appropriate for all colleges and universities, we recommend the following general strategies for strengthening education in the humanities at various kinds of institutions:

  —instruction in writing that is spread across the course of study;
  —courses integrating themes and subjects from the humanistic disciplines with each other and with other fields of study;

—clear sequences of courses in each of the disciplines of the humanities;

—use of resources from local cultural institutions;

—the development of new materials for teaching the humanities.

Until prior schooling meets the need, instruction in writing should be more thoroughly integrated with the entire undergraduate curriculum, through writing workshops supplementing majors in all fields of study or through sequences of requirements in writing. For at least a decade, parents, faculty, and employers have joined in deploring the inadequate writing skills of high school graduates and even students who have passed courses in college English. Many institutions have improved their programs in basic composition, many have created or revived learning centers to help students in reading and writing. But more needs to be done.

Students should write essays regularly in as many courses as possible and throughout the undergraduate years. Good writing in any field becomes more difficult as knowledge of the field leads to a specialized vocabulary and special modes of thought. The basic training offered in a freshman composition course should—but usually does not—suffice for upperclassmen in disciplines from anthropology to zoology. The teaching of writing must be the responsibility of all faculty, not only of English departments. Just as English faculty should not limit writing assignments to the subject of literature, faculty outside departments of English must consider the quality of writing in their normal evaluations of student work.

• At the University of Michigan, for example, the relatively new English Composition Board (ECB) coordinates a multi-leveled program in writing for all students and most departments in the college of liberal sciences and arts. The Board assesses a writing sample from each entering freshman and transfer student. According to the results, students are placed either in "special help" tutorials staffed by the Board or in introductory composition courses taught in the English department; some may be exempted from any required course. Every student, however, must take an upperclass writing course at some time after the sophomore year and before the final semester of undergraduate studies. These courses, normally taken in the student's major field and often taught by faculty from that field, explore the writing problems peculiar to each discipline. The Board offers faculty seminars for colleagues interested in creating upperclass writing courses in the various fields, and provides training for all faculty and graduate teaching assistants involved in the writing program. As noted in our chapter on the schools, ECB also offers help to regional high schools wanting to improve their instruction in composition.

The curriculum should include courses integrating various disciplines of the humanities with each other and with studies in other fields. In the early undergraduate years, such courses can effectively introduce students to the humanities by connecting humanistic studies with the students' own concerns; they can also stimulate students to take more courses in the humanities later on. At all levels, integrative courses allow students to explore the interrelationships among various kinds of knowledge and to gain perspective on a major field or chosen career.

Integrated approaches to the humanities may be particularly appropriate in two-year colleges, which now enroll more than half of all freshmen in the country. Two-year college students vary widely in academic preparation, educational goals, and cultural background. Some attend two-year colleges to prepare for matriculation in four-year institutions; others with shorter-term educational goals view the two-year curriculum as the extent of their formal education. Still others—young people, retired persons, and working adults of all ages—have goals ranging from vocational education to recreation and personal enrichment.

With this mix of purposes and constituencies, two-year institutions must be especially flexible and innovative in designing curricula in the humanities. According to the Center for the Study of Community Colleges, courses that integrate literature, art, history, and other subjects have proved particularly successful in recent years. The Center surveyed 178 institutions between 1975 and 1977; while enrollments in single-discipline courses in the humanities declined, the study showed, multidisciplinary courses grew in number and enrollments. As the Center observes, these latter courses represent "fertile ground for further exploration." Many are aimed at occupational and nontraditional students, for whom "the integrated approach affords an opportunity to maximize exposure to the humanities in a shorter time interval" (*The Humanities in Two-Year Colleges: Trends in Curriculum*, Los Angeles, 1978).

• *The Humanities in Two-Year Colleges* describes several integrative programs recently developed at two-year institutions. In some, a single theme or series of problems is studied from the perspectives of the humanities and other disciplines. Others blend contemporary popular culture with classic works of literature, philosophy, art, and music. For example, in a two-semester sequence developed jointly by three community college districts— Coast (of California), Chicago, and Miami-Dade—students proceed from the study of contemporary popular culture to an examination of the arts and humanities in historical perspective. Designed by nine humanists from various disciplines, the course can be taught either by an individual or in teams.

• The League for Innovation in the Community Colleges, a national consortium of fifty-two institutions, has encouraged several efforts to integrate the humanities with career education. At Moraine Valley Community College in Illinois, a course in design builds skills in human relations, writing, cultural understanding, and decision making. Nursing and business students at Johnson County Community College in Kansas explore ethical perspectives in occupational courses; the college's law enforcement training program includes studies in history. Johnson County is also developing a clearing house for information on strengthening the humanities in two-year institutions.

Four-year institutions can look back on a long tradition of integrative courses in the humanities, including the "Great Books" surveys found in general education after the First World War. Introductory surveys, if sufficiently probing, remain useful for acquainting lower division students with the humanities. However, education in the humanities should not be confined to the first year or two of a four-year curriculum. As the Carnegie

Foundation for the Advancement of Teaching has pointed out, students ought to have opportunities throughout their course of study to integrate their growing knowledge in various subjects *(Missions of the College Curriculum)*. These opportunities should include intermediate and advanced courses cutting across disciplines in the humanities, and courses connecting the humanities and arts with the sciences, social sciences, engineering, and communications. Courses relating the humanities to preprofessional studies should also be offered, in coherent sequences, throughout the undergraduate years.

• Under a grant from the Northwest Area Foundation, Hamline University in St. Paul, Minnesota, developed a cross-disciplinary program based on the study of values and moral choices. In a year-long course for freshmen, teams of faculty from various disciplines compare characteristic approaches to issues of value and choice. Students explore how the major academic fields have influenced each other and study classics from each field in their historical context. Students at all levels may take "course clusters" representing the perspectives of two or more disciplines on a common theme.

• With support from several private foundations and the National Endowment for the Humanities (NEH), the Department of Humanities at the University of Florida, Gainesville, has developed a program relating the humanities to seven professions including medicine, engineering, and business administration. After multidisciplinary core courses, preprofessional undergraduates take special courses exploring humanistic issues in greater depth.

Ideally, integrative courses should reveal relationships among areas of knowledge. Scholars have given us fascinating accounts of the connections between optics, geometry, and art in the fifteenth and sixteenth centuries; the philosophical foundations of science, mathematics, and religion from ancient Greece to the modern era; the reflection of public function and aesthetic preference in architecture and structural engineering; the social characteristics of particular geographic regions; and the tension between compartmentalization and synthesis of knowledge in any given historical period. At an increasing number of colleges and universities, often with support from the NEH and private foundations, new curricular programs have examined the interdependence of science, technology, and human values, or introduced ethics and other humanistic themes into programs of professional studies.

Courses combining several fields do not automatically evoke superior faculty wisdom or student comprehension. Indeed, the terms *interdisciplinary* and *team-taught* have acquired a mystique that may be misleading; they can disguise shoddy, ill-conceived courses that merely dilute a variety of subjects rather than unite them in any coherent or imaginative synthesis. Humanists are often reluctant to undertake a genuine exploration of cross-disciplinary problems and their social or ethical implications. In planning interdisciplinary courses, faculty often skirt the craggy terrain of intellectual and pedagogic assumptions and stay in the bureaucratic foothills of interdepartmental coordination. Such courses, if poorly conceived, may mislead students into believing that a superficial collection of facts about a variety of subjects is evidence of a depth of knowledge. On the other hand, there are courses in single disciplines where a genuine synthesis of various kinds of knowledge is nearly achieved by a teacher who has thought deeply about the relationships among disciplines.

In recommending integrative courses, we do not mean to diminish the importance of the traditional, discipline-based curriculum. No given course structure guarantees that students or faculty will discover new insights or pursue newly awakened interests. Integrative courses can introduce students to the disciplines of the humanities while connecting these with students' vocational or intellectual interests. But these courses should also encourage students to explore the regular curriculum of the humanities.

To help students choose wisely, the curriculum in the humanities should be arranged in clear sequences of courses taught at every level by the best faculty available. At many institutions, specialization has fragmented the humanities and narrowed the scope of separate courses, especially at the intermediate level. Often students must select from a catalog with few signposts to meaningful progressions from introductory to advanced courses and with few correlations among subject areas of each discipline. Senior faculty often shun lower division courses and sometimes teach upper division courses as if they were graduate seminars. In the humanities, no less than in other disciplines, some specialization is necessary for achieving depth of knowledge in the major field. Faculty must remember, however, that very few of even the most committed undergraduate majors will go on to graduate study in the humanities. Departments should look closely at the balance of majors and nonmajors who enroll in their courses, and ask whether their curriculum has become too diffuse or professionalized. The answer may well turn on the extent to which a subject offers insights that students can apply to other courses in and outside the discipline.

Undergraduate curricula in the humanities should include cooperative ventures with local cultural institutions. Many departments in the humanities can share resources with cultural institutions such as museums, libraries, historical societies, and theaters. Cooperative programs can expand the horizons of students, teachers, and staff. In preparing or teaching a course using museum materials, for example, museum staff can increase their knowledge of the cultural contexts of their collections and humanists can learn how artifacts might contribute to their subject fields and teaching techniques. Not all colleges and universities have access to a major museum or cultural institution, but many will find unsuspected treasures in their own backyards: a dig where students can learn the techniques of field archeology; a local historical organization or library with resources for historical research; a theater where students can see or perform dramatic literature.

• One model of cooperation was developed at the University of Michigan, Dearborn. In a course on American civilization between 1865 and 1914, students examined the humanities against the background of technological and material culture. University faculty in literature, art history, and the history of music joined with curators from the neighboring Henry Ford and Greenfield Village museums, combining lectures with tours of the museums and study of artifacts. Students rated nearly every aspect of the course as outstanding, and a museum staff member went on to offer a course in material culture for university credit.

New texts and educational materials should be developed for teaching the humanities. The paperback revolution, now more a familiar fact of life than a revolution, has benefited the academic humanities by enabling more students to own more books and helping the curriculum keep pace with knowledge. Computer, phototypesetting, and video readout technologies are increasing access to written materials and to learning still further. Whether through new technologies or more traditional means, we need educational materials integrating the humanities with vocational and preprofessional studies and introducing into humanistic studies themes from professional fields—for example, case studies in the ethical problems of doctors, lawyers, and engineers as a part of the curriculum in philosophy. Materials offering a view of the many cultural traditions in this country and abroad—for example, more and better translations of foreign literatures, ancient and modern—are needed. Foreign language and international studies suffer, in the words of the President's Commission, from "a lack of imaginative curricula dealing with other countries and cultures; and a similar lack of imaginative language-training courses." Noting that "foreign language instruction at any level should be a humanistic pursuit," the Commission has recommended more experimentation in foreign language instruction and in the integration of this instruction with cultural studies *(Strength Through Wisdom)*.

• Several recently developed interdisciplinary courses in the humanities have led to the creation of study guides, textbooks, and anthologies. Community colleges have been particularly active in mixing text with television in such courses as "The Ascent of Man." Many four-year institutions have adopted "The Art of Being Human," another text and course developed by community college humanists. As an example of integrating the humanities with the professions, the American Bar Association's Commission on Undergraduate Education in Law and the Humanities has commissioned scholars in history, literature, and philosophy to prepare essays, curriculum guides, and supporting documents. Although these materials will be useful in undergraduate law-related studies, their primary aim is to incorporate legal themes into courses in the humanities.

Students and teachers depend on publishers and libraries for the thousands of books they read in the humanities. Many of these are standard classics, widely used and available in reasonably priced editions from university and commercial publishers. Ways must be found to keep important titles in print when demand for them falls below a certain level. Superior translations of foreign literature, important older works of scholarship, minor works of major writers, works of significant new writers—though these often sell fewer copies than standard classics, they are no less important to education in the humanities. Academic libraries must make every effort to maintain adequate collections in the humanities. As the costs of materials and services have escalated and as students have turned increasingly to technical and career education, many libraries have reduced their budgets for acquisitions in the humanities. Whatever the mission of the institution, librarians and administrators should sustain collections that reflect an institutional commitment to learning in the humanities.

Strengthening the curriculum will require considerable human and financial resources. Many outside sources of support offer funds for curriculum and faculty development. The NEH's Division of Education Programs makes grants of various sizes for projects ranging from an experimental course to the overhaul of an entire curriculum. Less well known, perhaps, are grants from other federal agencies as well as associations and private foundations. These too vary in size and duration. The National Humanities Faculty has a small but promising new program to assist community colleges. The associations usually regrant modest funds provided by a major donor; for example, the Association of American Colleges offers up to ten thousand dollars to individual faculty members for "grassroots" experiments in the curriculum under its Quality in Liberal Learning program funded by the Ford Foundation. The federal Fund for the Improvement of Postsecondary Education (an office of the Department of Education) makes grants for curricular improvement and innovation in disciplinary and interdisciplinary studies. The Fund periodically publishes *Resources for Change* (Washington, D.C.) to encourage dissemination of the projects it has supported. Some associations, often with support from the NEH, sponsor conferences where faculty and administrators can exchange ideas.

Sources of support outside colleges and universities must supplement institutional efforts, but the primary obligation for invigorating the humanities belongs to undergraduate institutions themselves. They must use whatever resources they have, reallocating them where necessary to concentrate the faculty's energy on the curriculum. This is not a mechanical matter of raising average departmental enrollments, not a limited exercise in crisis management for the humanities. For all administrators, faculty, and students, the issue is fundamental: the reconstitution of liberal education as the best educational philosophy for this democracy.

The Commission on the Humanities of 1964 observed, "Students are no different from other people in that they can quickly observe where money is being made available and draw the logical conclusion as to which activities their society considers important" (*Report of the Commission on the Humanities*, New York, 1964). This has not changed. Behind the vocationalism that has narrowed undergraduate education is a job market that offers few rewards for a liberal education. Students are probably more responsive to trends in the job market and the biases of employers than to any statement of mission, however ringing, or any curriculum, whether time-honored or innovative. In the past few years, the job prospects of college graduates have recovered somewhat from the recession of the late 1960s and early 1970s; according to the College Placement Council, job offers to new recipients of the bachelor's degree in 1979 were up 30 percent over the previous year's level. The real increase, however, occurred in technical and professional fields. Liberal arts graduates, particularly those in the humanities and social sciences, remain at a disadvantage in the job market.

College placement services advise liberal arts students to acquire technical skills and knowledge along with their more general education. It is just as important for colleges to advise employers that a liberal education with solid grounding in the humanities cultivates technique as well as intellect. Many of today's employers are themselves liberally educated men and women; yet in hiring college graduates they underestimate such qualities as imagination, critical judgment, and sensitivity to values. Not only students, teachers, and administrators, but also employers must recognize that a humanistic education is invaluable for the trained technician.

GRADUATE EDUCATION FOR THE PROFESSIONS

The humanities have recently gained some visibility in professional education, and not by accident. The professions today face perplexing issues whose solutions are not quantifiable or easy to find. Many professionals find themselves suspect in the eyes of a public that demands accountability from experts it formerly trusted. In giving physicians new powers over human death and disease, biomedical technology does not reconcile the "ought" of ethics with the "is" of the clinic. Lawyers and public administrators are often caught in the glare of controversy over issues of public policy and in the civil feuds of an unprecedentedly litigious citizenry. In a complex international economy, men and women in business must negotiate in unfamiliar languages and cultures, while at home they are asked to weigh profit against social responsibility. Alert to the value of humanistic perspectives on these issues, some educators in the professions have sought the contributions that history, literature, foreign languages, and philosophy can make to the training of future professionals.

Ironically, the policies of professional schools often conflict with their efforts to integrate the humanities with professional education. As many as half of all undergraduates plan to undertake some post-baccalaureate study. Competition is keen for places in professional schools. Like the preferences of employers, the admission practices of these schools have a powerful influence on how undergraduates shape their course of study. The "pre-med syndrome" of recent years is a deplorable example of this kind of influence. Commission member Dr. Lewis Thomas has commented,

> The influence of the modern medical school on liberal-arts education in this country over the last decade has been baleful and malign, nothing less. The admission policies of the medical schools are at the root of the trouble. If something is not done quickly to change those policies, all the joy of going to college will have been destroyed, not just for that growing majority of undergraduate students who draw breath only to become doctors, but for everyone else—all the students and all the faculty members, as well.
>
> The medical schools used to say they wanted applicants as broadly educated as possible, and they used to mean it. . . .
>
> There is still some talk in medical deans' offices about the need for general culture, but nobody really means it. . . . ("How to Fix the Premedical Curriculum," *New England Journal of Medicine*, 25 May 1978)

Dr. Thomas's point is true of educational policy in other professions as well. Preprofessionalism has had severe effects on undergraduate life and learning. More disturbing are the effects that preprofessionalism may have on the standards of professionalism itself. Doctors, lawyers, and businessmen and women who pass over the liberal arts in a premature quest for expertise are not likely to be better professionals. Indeed they will probably be less capable than colleagues whose professional training rests, in Dr. Thomas's words, on "the bedrock of knowledge about our civilization."

RECOMMENDATION 13:   We recommend that joint conferences of professionals, professional school administrators and faculty, and humanists be convened to discuss the kinds of preparation in the humanities that professional schools should expect of their applicants and graduates. Participants and sponsors for these conferences should include such organizations as the American Assembly of Collegiate Schools of Business, the Association of American Law Schools, and the Association of American Medical Colleges, as well as public and private agencies with an interest in the humanities in professional education.

Professional schools' obligation to undergraduate education is commensurate with their influence on the undergraduate course of study. If they believe, as increasingly they seem to, that the humanities are an important part of professional training, they ought to require applicants to have substantial background in the humanities. The integration of the humanities with professional education must build upon a foundation of knowledge gained in undergraduate study; otherwise, it is likely to be remedial and ineffectual.

Graduate professional study should include courses providing humanistic perspectives on every phase of professional training. Well-designed individual courses on "Ethics in . . ." or "The Professional Responsibilities of . . . ," now fairly common, can be instructive; but if these are random and belated, as is often the case, they do a disservice to the professional degree candidates whom they purport to educate. As Daniel Callahan and Sissela Bok observed, following an extended survey of the place of ethics in higher education,

> In practically every professional school, courses on ethics are considered peripheral to the curriculum and teachers often have no special qualifications. Moreover, those who teach ethics rarely gain professional rewards for their efforts; it is often a personal commitment, well outside the mainstream of status and prestige. ("The Role of Applied Ethics in Learning," *Change*, September 1979)

Nor, we would add, does an exclusive preoccupation with professional ethics take advantage of the many ways that the humanities can better a professional's life and work.

• With support from private foundations and the NEH, several institutions have begun to blend the humanities with professional studies. Through its Interface Program, for example, the Commonwealth Fund has made major grants for the reexamination and reform of the premedical and preclinical years of medical education at seven institutions: Boston University, Brown University, the University of Chicago, Dartmouth College and Medical School, Duke University, the Johns Hopkins University, and the University of Rochester. The scope of reform varies among these institutions. In every instance the major objective is to improve medical education by such means as eliminating the redundancy of undergraduate and medical school science courses. However, as the Fund's description of the Interface Program emphasizes, a major benefit of revising premedical and medical education is to broaden the education of physicians:

> Every institution supported under the Interface Program must concern itself with the "premedical syndrome." An astonishingly large percentage of the students entering college each year are intent upon a medical career. They load their schedules with courses in the natural sciences and mathematics, often well beyond those necessary for admission to medical school. . . . In too many cases, premedical students themselves treat humanities and social sciences as strictly secondary. . . . *(1978 Annual Report)*

• The Interface Program enables students to combine their professional training with serious study of the humanities, social sciences, and other disciplines.

• Integration of the humanities with professional education has been a priority of the NEH's Division of Education Programs for some years. The Endowment provided substantial support, for example, for the development of a Department of Humanities in the College of Medicine at Pennsylvania State University in Hershey. Since the college opened its doors in 1967, the department has offered seminars combining literature, philosophy, religion, and political science with medical students' clinical studies. A course called "Dying, Death, and Grief" includes fiction, biography, religious literature, clinical material, and interviews with dying patients.

• With NEH support, the Claremont Graduate School developed a pilot series of courses in the humanities for its Management and Policy program. Comprising one of seven areas in the program's core curriculum, the humanities' offerings include philosophy, history, and literature.

The continued development of a role for the humanities in graduate education for the professions will require the involvement of individual humanists and their departments. It often seems that professional school faculty are more eager than their colleagues in the humanities to discuss common goals and to pool resources. Humanists should give more consideration to how their disciplines overlap with the professions; faculty and the administrators who determine incentives should regard professional education as a legitimate extension of the capabilities of departments in the humanities.

GRADUATE TRAINING IN THE HUMANITIES

Current discussions of graduate education take place in the shadow of the job crisis confronting young Ph.D.'s. Gloomy statistics and predictions abound, the darkest of which relate to the humanities, where advanced training has traditionally led almost exclusively into college teaching. The academic job prospects for today's Ph.D.'s in the humanities seem dismal indeed, especially in contrast to the prosperous period of higher education that followed the Second World War and lasted into the 1970s. Particularly in the years following Sputnik, soaring college enrollments, large federal expenditures on university-based research, and a generally favorable economic climate encouraged doctoral study in most of the arts and sciences, including the humanities. According to the Commission on Human Resources of the National Research Council, the number of Ph.D.'s awarded in the humanities rose from 3,210 in 1968 to 5,364 in the peak year of 1973—an increase of over 60 percent in five years. Of all Ph.D.'s in the humanities conferred in the United States since 1920, more than 25 percent were awarded in the 1960s and over 44 percent in the 1970s (*Science, Engineering, and Humanities Doctorates in the United States: 1977 Profile*, Washington, D.C., 1978; and *Employment of Humanities Ph.D.'s: A Departure from Traditional Jobs*, Washington, D.C., 1980).

Insofar as academic job opportunities depend on the growth of undergraduate enrollments, the new Ph.D.'s of the early 1970s might have expected to find jobs—between 1967 and 1975, enrollments grew steadily from just under 7 million to nearly 11.3 million. In fact, however, there was a sharp turn for the worse in the academic labor market. Faculties in the humanities leveled off, college and university budgets began to feel the pinch of inflation, and undergraduates started taking fewer courses in the humanities. In a report to the National Board on Graduate Education in 1975, David Breneman noted "the mood of despair" in university English departments that had difficulty placing new Ph.D.'s. Two highly rated departments had placed only seven out of twenty-one and eleven of fifty of their students seeking jobs in 1974, and many of the successful ones had found only one-year, terminal appointments. At the same time, Breneman noted, graduate applications in the humanities showed little decline despite growing publicity about the shortage of jobs (*Graduate School Adjustments to the "New Depression" in Higher Education*, Washington, D.C.). Soon, however, the shortage of jobs did begin to affect graduate education in the humanities. By 1978, the last year for which complete figures are available, the number of doctorates awarded had decreased to 4,235. Total applications for graduate programs in the humanities have declined over the past few years.

For young humanists today the circumstances are disheartening. Many who obtain teaching posts have little realistic hope for tenure, for a "buyers' market" among academic employers—coupled with austere departmental budgets and uncertainties about future enrollments—has led to frequent use of short-term, nontenurable contracts and has created a growing number of academic nomads.

Forecasts of the future academic job market vary, since they depend on such variables as student enrollment patterns and the number of Ph.D.'s awarded. There is little ground for optimism, however. Two things seem clear. First, higher education's era of spectacular growth is over, and there will be reduced demand for new college teachers for at least a decade. Second, faculties have emerged from the era of growth top-heavy with tenured professors. This imbalance and a higher mandatory retirement age will further reduce the opportunities available to young Ph.D.'s. A study by the American Council on Education estimated that age-seventy retirement laws would result in almost two-thirds fewer faculty job openings from 1983 to 1990 than under current retirement policies (Thomas Corwin and Paula Knepper, "Finance and Employment Implications of Raising the Mandatory Retirement Age for Faculty," Washington, D.C., 1978). Some observers predict that the job crisis will subside in the 1990s, when a substantial number of the present faculty will retire. Others contend that if graduate schools continue to award doctorates at present rates, in 1995 the new Ph.D. in the humanities will have a one-in-six chance of finding an academic post.

There is a need for complete, consolidated information on Ph.D. enrollments, current unemployment and employment prospects, and kinds of training that Ph.D. candidates have or should have. Projections of the need for Ph.D.'s in the next decade vary widely, partly because vital bits of information are missing. For example, what is the impact on the job market of recent recipients of the Ph.D. who have not obtained academic jobs or who fail to achieve tenure in their initial appointment? How many decide to stay in nonacademic jobs and how many, hanging on in marginal jobs, compete with the newest graduates for the few academic positions that become available? The National Research Council's *Employment of Humanities Ph.D.'s: A Departure From Traditional Jobs,* which documents some recent shifts in patterns of employment, ought to help graduate departments, learned associations, and young humanists plan for the future. We hope that further studies now planned by the Council—on Ph.D.'s in nonacademic jobs and how their training relates to their work—will begin to show how best to use the talents of humanists who cannot find teaching positions.

In the meantime, there is little consensus on what to do. In our own deliberations as a Commission, we too have disagreed on how graduate education should adjust to the shortage of jobs. On the one hand, we believe that some graduate programs in the humanities should lessen their emphasis on scholarly research and increase the preparation for teaching or for nonacademic jobs. On the other hand, the continuity of humanistic scholarship requires that some institutions concentrate on scholarly training. In either case, groups of universities should consider consortium arrangements, based on particular institutional strengths and regional convenience, as a way of maintaining graduate programs at a reduced level. The missions and resources of graduate schools vary no less than those of undergraduate institutions. Not all will adjust in the same way to the new climate surrounding higher education, nor should they. All graduate schools, however, should warn applicants of the difficulty of finding teaching positions. Graduate programs in the humanities that cannot offer students reasonable prospects of employment, whether academic or nonacademic, should be abolished.

RECOMMENDATION 14:   We recommend that graduate schools and departments reassess their purposes and curricula, and consider how the training they offer in the humanities might be better adapted to both academic and nonacademic employment.

Over the last decade, more and more Ph.D.'s in the humanities have gone to work outside the academy—a trend that is likely to continue as long as there is a shortage of teaching jobs. Yet neither graduate faculty nor their students have responded realistically to changed prospects for employment. According to Lewis Solmon, many faculty are not well informed about the various labor markets open to graduate candidates; particularly in the humanities, he has found, few faculty look upon job preparation as part of their role (*Alternative Careers for Humanities PhDs,* New York, 1979). Most graduate students apparently still expect to find teaching jobs; since the early 1970s, despite the well-known severity of the job shortage, the percentage of Ph.D. candidates who plan exclusively on academic employment has declined only slightly.

Some educators advise graduate students to take courses in other fields, including business. They argue that graduate students should plan on—and be seen to have planned on—a nonacademic career. They suggest that students should consult campus place-ment services throughout their graduate careers in order to stay abreast of changing employment possibilities and the skills they will need to develop in tandem with their usual graduate studies. This argument should not be taken to extremes. We see no reason why a student should pursue a Ph.D. in the humanities to prepare for a career in banking. On the other hand—and this should be true whatever the state of the job market—graduate schools should encourage students to assess their prospects for employment and prepare for a specific career path, whether in college teaching, research, educational or public administration, school teaching, or cultural preservation.

• The academic job shortage has already given rise to some creative experiments in the graduate curriculum. In history, for example, over forty programs in public and applied historical studies train students to adapt historical research methods to problems of public policy, corporate archives, and local and municipal history. The Philosophy Department at Bowling Green State University places master's degree candidates in internships where they use skills gained through studying philosophy to examine problems of public policy and administration. Some private foundations and the NEH support projects adapting graduate training to nonacademic employment. Many learned societies have stepped up their efforts to inform members about nontraditional labor markets and how graduate curricula might adjust to them.

We would caution that the preparation of students for nonacademic careers should not be based on mere curricular artifice. Particularly when preparing for jobs in museums, historical preservation, or archives, students should have practical experience (through internships, for example); their teachers should have had solid training or experience themselves in such fields. To offer superficial crash courses is to serve students poorly. It is also to lose an opportunity for the humanities to transcend an emergency mentality by undertaking a genuinely creative reexamination of their own methods, assumptions, and importance.

Doctoral and master's degree programs might offer specific preparation for teaching in two-year colleges, and should consult them on what they need. These institutions, understandably unwilling to become dumping grounds for surplus doctorates who would rather teach elsewhere, would like to see graduate schools provide the kind of training necessary for teaching in community colleges. A number of programs, including the Doctor of Arts programs in English departments at the University of Virginia and the University of Michigan and the graduate program in history at Princeton University, have successfully used community college internships as a part of graduate training. The recently established Community College Humanities Association can help coordinate such efforts at collaboration between universities and two-year colleges.

Graduate education must train students in the specialized research required for the thesis or dissertation. Graduate study should also insure breadth of knowledge. As teachers, or as nonacademic humanists, many Ph.D.'s will act as brokers between specialized knowledge and the interests of students and the broader public. Good teachers are generalists in their own and adjacent disciplines. Advanced study should encourage students to look critically at the subject each will teach—at its assumptions, methods, and relationship to the sciences, social sciences, and public life. All graduate programs in the humanities should include training in the teaching of writing. Graduate departments of foreign languages should offer thorough preparation in the teaching of beginning and intermediate language courses; the majority of their graduates, if they are fortunate enough to get academic jobs, will have to do at least some such teaching.

The continued vitality of the humanities depends on the successful adjustment of graduate education to the job crisis. Some programs will scale down as applications diminish. Some departments will offer training for the new kinds of jobs available. Whatever the duration of the crisis, however, we must argue the compelling need for continuous support of graduate education in the humanities. In every discipline, knowledge is found and refined in the exchange of ideas. Perhaps especially for the humanities, our universities—with their outstanding scholars and library holdings—provide the richest medium for this exchange, and graduate education the most certain guarantee of continued intellectual vigor. Particularly if the shortage of academic jobs should subside in the 1990s, it is important that the humanities attract outstanding undergraduates in the 1980s. A major interruption in the flow of talent through our graduate schools would jeopardize the continuity, and thus the quality, of education and scholarship in the humanities.

Our society must and can afford adequate financial support for graduate students. At the same time that the cost of graduate education has risen dramatically, funds have dried up for the support of graduate study in the arts and sciences. The Woodrow Wilson Fellowships have disappeared and the Danforth Foundation's fellowship program soon will. Support for minority graduate students has declined; for example, the Ford Foundation has reduced its once generous aid. Many funding agencies, notably the National Science Foundation, have set assistance levels below the full cost of graduate study, thus burdening hard-pressed university budgets and graduate students with additional costs. Reduced federal support for advanced study in the sciences may further shift institutional resources away from the humanities as universities take up the slack in support of science programs.

Teaching assistantships can cover part of the cost of graduate study while enlarging the experience of students. But teaching and other wage-earning activities should not seriously impede advancement toward a graduate degree. Nor should graduate students have to incur enormous debts that cannot soon be repaid from beginning salaries that are now scandalously low in humanistic fields—from 1969 to 1979, the typical starting salary for an assistant professor of English rose from about $10,000 to $15,000 in current dollars, but inflation reduced the latter salary to about $7,500 in constant 1969 dollars. Advanced research, usually a prerequisite for the Ph.D. dissertation, often requires the student to travel some distance to find essential materials; yet few dollars are available for travel or dissertation subsidies.

There is no national program of graduate fellowships for advanced students in the humanities. We think there should be. In 1974 the National Board on Graduate Education recommended that federally funded merit fellowships for graduate study be extended to all academic disciplines. The Board proposed that the NEH administer a counterpart to the National Science Foundation's fellowship program and recommended an additional two thousand portable, three-year federal awards (*Federal Policy Alternatives Toward Graduate Education,* Washington, D.C.). A similar recommendation appeared in the report by fifteen university presidents, *Research Universities and the National Interest* (New York, 1978), which noted, "It is surely in the national interest to support and encourage high achievement in every domain of intellectual endeavor. Extending the merit fellowship program to humanistic fields would . . . demonstrate that the national interest in graduate education is not limited to science and technology." Recently, the Sloan Commission on Government and Higher Education has proposed a program of three thousand federal merit scholarships for graduate study in all academic disciplines. As our own report went to press, Congress was considering two proposals for federal support of graduate study: a National Graduate Fellows Program of portable merit fellowships in the arts, humanities, and social sciences; and a program of National Talent Grants, to be administered by institutions, for exceptionally needy first-year graduate students. We urge Congress to take favorable action on these proposals.

The strength of our graduate schools is hard won. We are confident that, with characteristic resilience, graduate education in the humanities will adapt to changed employment prospects for Ph.D.'s and indeed other circumstances in the decades to come. Looking beyond the job shortage or any other crisis, universities, private foundations, and the federal government must help graduate training in the humanities uphold its traditional purpose: to prepare especially gifted students to be outstanding scholars and teachers in their fields.

RESEARCH AND SCHOLARSHIP

Research in the humanities has flourished in recent decades. Each major branch of the humanities has developed new methods for criticism and interpretation, sometimes borrowing from other disciplines and often opening up new fields of inquiry. Using paradigms from linguistics and anthropology, for example, literary scholars have developed a science of signs for analyzing the social and psychological significance of texts; the very notion of what constitutes a text has been expanded. The field of political and social philosophy has grown, and philosophers have helped map terrain in the behavioral sciences. The comparative study of religions has provided useful models for comparative studies in general. Interdisciplinary research in American and area studies has spread. Using demographic data and methods from social science, social historians have drawn attention to the common people and how they have lived.

Imaginative and solid scholarly activity in the humanities must be sustained in the years to come. The future of humanistic research will depend on how successfully the entire system of scholarly production and dissemination—scholars, academic institutions, libraries, research centers, publishers and learned journals, and foundations and other sources of support —solves problems created by the growth of scholarship and indeed of knowledge itself.

The expansion of higher education, libraries, and faculties over the past three decades has stimulated a proportionate increase in the amount and quality of American humanistic research. The sheer volume of research threatens to inundate libraries, scholars, students, and the reading public with unmanageable masses of printed matter. For scholarly presses and libraries, the proliferation of materials raises urgent questions of what shall be published and purchased, how it shall be stored, and who shall read it. New technologies of microprocessing and communications can help solve problems in the management of scholarly information. The National Enquiry into Scholarly Communication has recently focused attention on uses of technology in the production, transmission, storage, and retrieval of research materials. New technologies also promise to transform scholarly activity itself, and in some cases the material form of its results, in significant ways. Technology affects old forms of inquiry and expression, and it will surely create new ones. It will shape the ways people pursue literature, history, philosophy, and other subjects. As use of the new technologies increases, humanists must share responsibility for insuring that the use is rational, open, and productive.

Computers and their software can assist scholarship. To many scholars in the humanities, computers represent quantification and seem to require forbidding expertise in programming, design, and interpretation. With relatively modest skills, however, and without the quantitative methods of social science, humanists can use computers to increase the accuracy and completeness of their scholarly work. Computers offer an efficient and reliable tool for comparative analysis of texts, composing and editing, and publishing. With computers a scholar can rapidly retrieve information in printout or video readout form from bibliographic and factual data bases, books and articles, or indeed from other scholars.

Scientists and social scientists have built data bases of scientific, historical, political, and social information. Humanists can tap these convenient resources for interdisciplinary study. In their own disciplines, humanists can electronically compile and consult dictionaries, indexes, and bibliographies.

• Among learned societies, the Modern Language Association (MLA) leads in the exploration of computer-aided research. Supported by the National Endowment for the Humanities (Division of Research Grants—Research Tools Program), the MLA has published the *MLA International Bibliography* (available through Lockheed's DIALOG system) and with help from the Andrew W. Mellon Foundation is studying new methods of indexing and retrieving bibliographic information. The Center for Computer Assisted Textual Analysis (at the University of California, San Diego) plans to develop an archive of machine-readable texts in modern languages, and has links with other language centers. The Classics Department at the University of California, Irvine, is using computers to compile a thesaurus of ancient Greek.

Convenience, accuracy, and access to nonhumanistic disciplines are not the computer's only benefits to humanists. Technology can free scholars' time for analysis, interpretation, and appreciation, giving them the opportunity to write essays for broad audiences. With evidence available on computer in the library through codes in an essay's appendix, footnotes could guide readers to supporting information stored and retrievable in a new mode. This practice is especially suitable for scholarship in which the humanities and social sciences intersect—where the assembly of data is needed to support humanistic argument in, for example, economic and social history, the history and philosophy of science, and linguistics. In these and other fields, technology enables humanists to return to the ideal of writing interpretive essays for the general reader in which high literary quality is possible because of easy separate access to the mass of data.

In the distribution of resources for humanistic study, the revolution in communications is a necessity. Without new technologies, which themselves increase the volume of information and the means of handling it, compatibility between the preservation and the accessibility of materials would be impossible to maintain.

Computer and duplicating technologies assist scholarly communication. Computers and phototypesetters can accelerate the preparation, publication, and distribution of scholarly materials to individuals or libraries and other institutions. Computers enable libraries to compile bibliographic information and to supplement it through networks such as the RLG/RLIN and OCLC; the Library of Congress, for example, plans to make its vast bibliographies available to others. Libraries can share their resources through computer cataloging and electronic modes such as tele-electronic copying and the transmission of images on cathode-ray equipment. The storage and retrieval of already published sources is provided by such data systems as LEXIS and DIALOG. These technologies expand the individual's access to library materials and extend access to more people, including many from outside academic institutions—a step that many research libraries have already taken as public demand increases and budgets for public libraries are cut back.

As new technologies change the functions of research libraries, however, they also raise questions about the scholarly use of library materials. How, for example, will users' expectations change as bibliographic tools change? What impact will selective acquisitions or electronic storage and retrieval have on the working methods of scholars?

Indeed the rapid growth of informational technologies raises many questions. How can machines be used and access to materials be extended without infringing copyright? Can libraries, university presses, and scholarly journals achieve economies without depreciating their services to faculty and students? Who gains and who loses as the storage and delivery systems of journals and other materials become centralized? Who will decide what gets published in any form, and who will select what libraries should preserve and what economies they should make? What is the effectiveness and economic feasibility of different technological processes? Who will subsidize presses whose expenses exceed net sales, or journals whose circulation drops? What place do fees and royalties have in the world of printouts and readouts?

The partial list of organizations or groups that have begun to answer such questions is impressive: the Association of Research Libraries (ARL); the American Library Association; the National Commission on Libraries and Information Science; the National Science Foundation; the Council on Library Resources; the National Commission on New Technological Uses of Copyrighted Works (CONTU, which submitted its final report in July 1978); the Library of Congress; the Center for Research Libraries; the Research Library Group (and other consortia or networks); the Authors Guild; the Association of American University Presses (AAUP); the Association of American Publishers; the American Council of Learned Societies (ACLS); the National Enquiry into Scholarly Communication.

In its report, the National Enquiry recommends the establishment of a "linked, national bibliographic system," a national periodicals center, a national library agency, an office of scholarly communication within the National Endowment for the Humanities, and a standing committee (jointly sponsored by ACLS, AAUP, and ARL) "composed of scholars, publishers, and librarians for continuing discussion of the nature and direction of technological change in the system of scholarly communication" (*Scholarly Communication: The Report of the National Enquiry*, Baltimore, 1979).

We share the Enquiry's conviction that the revolution in communications should not be allowed to overshadow the human values to be served: "Technologists must understand that humanistic scholarship is not merely information or data and that its human character must somehow be transmitted through the medium of the machine." We join the many groups who, like the National Enquiry, want to get on with the work of developing a national bibliographic system and a national periodicals center. The National Endowment for the Humanities already supports scholarly publishing and projects in library automation. While it does not plan to set up a specific office for the purpose, the Endowment will improve its capabilities in the area of scholarly communication. With support from private foundations, the Enquiry's proposed committee for monitoring and directing technology into important areas has been set up by the ACLS. Its membership includes scholars, librarians, publishers, and technicians. We suggest that this committee regularly consult other constituencies as well, such as university administrators, students, and the NEH. Among the committee's many tasks should be the continuing analysis of uses, costs, and needs; and the discussion of what kinds of journals, modes, and incentives could encourage scholars to write interpretive essays separated from the scaffolding of data.

Humanists must play a major role in stating the objectives and controlling the applications of informational technology. Currently, the influence of scholars, teachers, and students in the humanities on the uses of technology is negligible. This is not surprising, for most humanists are concerned with the idea, the document, the manuscript, and the published work much more than with the processes by which scholarship is produced and distributed. Many assume that computers serve only the research needs of scientists, social scientists, and engineers. We urge humanists to learn technology's capabilities so they can employ it, describe its limitations, manage its uses, and ultimately guide its course. Above all, humanists should participate in such cooperative mechanisms of control as the ACLS committee. By so doing, they will insure that important qualitative issues are discussed: criteria for sorting, evaluating, and using information; the proper balance between access and other individual rights; and the different ways that scholars from many disciplines define fact, accuracy, and error.

As a beginning, we suggest three guidelines concerning the uses of informational technology. First, constraints on access to bibliographic information should be eliminated worldwide. A world dependent on information cannot tolerate a new category of "haves" and "have-nots." Second, information in the humanities, as in other fundamental disciplines, should transcend national boundaries. The application of technology to improve the transnational flow of information will benefit scholars' work and will reduce intellectual and cultural isolation. Third, humanists should insure that new technologies add to, not reduce, our methods for using the record of human achievement.

Humanistic research will require support from many sources. For university and independent research libraries, the new technologies are not an unqualified boon. They cannot solve, though they may help control, the problem of basic operating expenses that has hit libraries particularly hard because increases in the costs of energy, paper, and other library materials have exceeded the rate of inflation. Computers cannot reverse the deterioration of books, a massive national problem threatening to reduce to dust within our lifetime perhaps half of the 227 million volumes held by research libraries. These libraries are the foundation for humanistic research. Their mission goes beyond service to the institution that, in the case of university libraries, pays most of their costs. University and independent research libraries serve the nation, and support for them is in the national interest. We recommend that federal funding under Title IIC of the Higher Education Act, which amounts to $6 million in fiscal year (FY) 1980, be raised to the authorized ceiling of $20 million by FY1982.

The homes of libraries and scholars, our colleges and universities are by far the most constant sources of support for scholarship in the humanities. As these institutions—and the public agencies and boards of trustees that govern them—reassess faculty responsibilities in a period of declining enrollments and economic stringency, we urge them not to cut back on the sabbatical time and financial resources that allow teachers to be scholars as well. We emphasize the importance of their sustaining young scholars through a period of limited academic job opportunities, lest the continuity of humanistic scholarship be jeopardized. Two-year colleges have a growing obligation to support the scholarly life of their faculties in the humanities. Humanists at these institutions are hampered in their efforts to pursue research interests; some teachers have had to resign their posts in order to accept grants for independent study. No state legislature, no governing board, no college or university should neglect the reinforcement that scholarship gives to teaching.

Research institutes and centers—such as the National Humanities Center, the Institute for Advanced Study at Princeton, the Center for Advanced Study in the Behavioral Sciences at Stanford, the Society for the Humanities at Cornell, and the Institute for Research in the Humanities at the University of Wisconsin, Madison—serve humanistic scholarship in valuable ways. They provide a nonhierarchical setting for dialogue among older and younger humanists. Through seminars and colloquia, they allow more sustained communication among scholars in various disciplines than is possible at many colleges and universities. They provide a climate for study undisturbed by the day-to-day pressures that scholars often face at their academic institutions. The outstanding collections of independent research libraries (such as the Huntington, Morgan, Newberry, and New York Public libraries) and of museums draw scholars from all over the world, affording opportunities for American and foreign humanists to share their ideas. Some research libraries, such as the Folger Shakespeare Library, have developed cooperative institutes to serve the research interests of faculty and graduate students from several surrounding universities.

The uniqueness of these institutions derives in part from their modest size and the collegiality it affords. They suffer from some of the same financial constraints as universities. Nevertheless, they should consider how they might serve the scholarly needs of more humanists, if possible by expanding the number of research positions they make available to scholars. Through postdoctoral and mid-career fellowships, for example, they could help young humanists. Support from parent universities, private foundations, and government agencies should at least remain at present levels and, if at all possible, should expand.

The academic system of rewards will have to recognize the new kinds of scholarly achievement made possible by informational technologies. What impact technology will have on the quality of scholarship is under debate; by allowing speedier publication of large quantities of scholarly work, new technologies may also eliminate the process by which additions to humanistic knowledge have always been screened. Assuming adequate processes of review for scholarship published in new modes, committees of appointment and promotion must be willing to consider, say, an electronic printout as part of a scholar's dossier. They should also view essays (published separately from their supporting data) as legitimate and sometimes preferable alternatives to monographs.

Of the outlets for publication of humanistic scholarship, learned journals are the most heterogeneous, ranging from newsletters to handsomely produced quarterlies. They number more than twenty-five hundred, about half in the humanities and social sciences. Some are supported by universities or colleges, others by learned societies or commercial publishers; still others are labors of love for scholars sharing a common interest. Their limited circulation and dependence on outside sources of support make the existence of many journals precarious indeed. Many nonacademics and some scholars see journals as "publishing mills" run chiefly to advance academic careers. Other scholars view journals as "closed shops" defining fields too narrowly or delaying editorial decisions for unconscionable periods of time. Certainly the growth in the number of journals over the last two decades—a 114 percent increase in four major humanistic disciplines between 1960 and 1975—has added to the budgetary problems of research libraries: between 1970 and 1976, expenditures on serials rose from 32 to 46 percent of the total acquisitions budgets of 119 libraries, while the portion spent on books decreased from 63 to 47 percent *(Scholarly Communication)*.

The learned journals remain invaluable for the dissemination of knowledge in the humanities. Particularly in interdisciplinary studies and fledgling subdisciplines, journals are a primary means of

communication among scholars and between scholars and interested general readers. Their major problem in the future will be
funding, particularly to the degree that automation and resource
sharing enable libraries to reduce serial acquisitions. The National
Enquiry observes that a reduction in library subscriptions will force
journals "to seek new markets, new sources of revenue, and new
ways of publishing that reduce costs" *(Scholarly Communication).*
We suggest that some journals might find all three by devoting
more space to general or synthetic essays of interest to scholars
from many disciplines and to the general reader. Journals such as
Daedalus and *The American Scholar* have already gained a wide
readership by publishing essays of broad appeal.

The chief publishers of book-length studies in the humanities
are of course the university presses, which have one foot on the
campus and the other in the world of commerce. Their fortunes
over the past three decades have paralleled, in some respects, those
of higher education. Roughly from the end of the Second World
War to the late 1960s, university presses prospered and nearly
doubled in number. During the same period, the total output of
titles by the entire American publishing industry more than
tripled. After about 1970, however, university and commercial
presses suffered a decline in sales. For the past decade, university
presses have felt the financial pinch on their parent institutions,
changes in libraries' policies of acquisition, and such general
economic factors as the rising costs of paper, production, and
distribution. Some have been forced out of existence.

The mission of the university press is scholarly, its clientele
chiefly academic. Unable to tap large commercial markets,
university presses rely on subsidies from the institutions they serve
and other sources. In the late 1950s and early 1960s, the Ford
Foundation granted nearly $3 million to a group of presses for
scholarship in the humanities and social sciences; in the 1970s, the
Andrew W. Mellon Foundation gave substantially for similar
purposes. The NEH has increased its support of scholarly publishing; it now makes subventions to university presses of up to $10,000
per work. Such subsidies must continue from various sources—private foundations, government agencies, and perhaps also universities without presses, as suggested by the National Enquiry—if the

dissemination of scholarship in the humanities is to keep up with its production. The NEH has also made Challenge Grants to a few university presses, but the three-to-one matching requirement is particularly difficult for institutions like presses that lack any natural or established constituency of support.

Aside from materials for research and outlets for publishing, the single greatest need of scholars in the humanities is for time. Time means weekends, summers, and sabbaticals; it requires money in the form of fellowships, grants, and stipends. Private foundations have long provided such support, recognizing both the intellectual and social value of humanistic research. For at least a decade, however, shrinking or stable endowments have combined with high rates of inflation to impose new limits on some of the best-known fellowship programs. Between 1968 and 1977, for example, the total cost of the Guggenheim Foundation's prestigious fellowship program doubled as the amount of each award increased to offset inflation, but the number of fellowships awarded rose only slightly. Added to the effects of inflation, the weakness of the dollar abroad has since 1964 considerably reduced the number of Fulbright-Hays Awards for Research Abroad in the humanities.

Thorough evidence is lacking on the changing amounts of support for fellowships in the humanities. Some representative figures are available, however. According to the Foundation Center, private foundation support for fellowships in all fields declined in current dollars from $38 million in 1975 to $29 million ($23.9 million in 1975 dollars) in 1978; or, expressed as fractions of the total dollars granted by foundations, from 5.6 to 3.5 percent. Statistics compiled by the Guggenheim Foundation for the period from 1968 to 1977 (*Reports of the President and the Treasurer, 1977*, New York) show an increase in the number of senior fellowships awarded in all fields by private sources, federal agencies, and centers for advanced study (43 percent over the decade). But most of this increase happened by 1973 and was offset by an even greater rise in the number of applications received (60 percent over ten years). Moreover, the average amount of individual grants increased at barely half the rate of inflation.

The Foundation Center's categories do not show clear trends in support for fellowships *in the humanities,* nor do they distinguish between fellowships for research and for other purposes. The Guggenheim Foundation's statistics cover only senior fellowships and do not distinguish among research fields. Still, we can draw two general conclusions from such evidence. First, the total number of fellowships for research in the humanities leveled off around 1973–74 and has declined since then in the case of some major private sources of support. Second, the purchasing power of the average grant has declined.

Except for the Rockefeller Foundation, which established a fellowship program in 1974, the NEH is the only major funding source to have significantly increased its direct support for fellowships in the humanities since 1973. In 1979 the Endowment's Division of Fellowships awarded nearly four hundred fellowships of different types for advanced study and research. Since 1974 it has also provided some funds for the fellowship programs of independent research libraries, centers, and the American Council of Learned Societies. In addition, the NEH's Division of Research Grants supports collaborative research projects in the development of primary research materials, editing and translation, and conferences designed to identify particular needs for basic humanistic research.

The NEH's support of humanistic research has been timely and generous. As private philanthropic support has declined, however, scholars have placed a greater and greater burden on the Endowment's resources: increases in the number of grants made by its Fellowship and Research Divisions have been more than equaled by increases in the number of applications these programs receive each year. We probably cannot expect the financial resources of the Endowment to grow as fast in the future as they have in the past. Moreover, the hard times ahead for higher education will probably create new pressures on all agencies of support.

RECOMMENDATION 15: Federal agencies and private foundations must increase their commitment to support the interlocking parts of the system of research and scholarship in the humanities. We recommend that the major sources of support for fellowships (NEH, Fulbright, Guggenheim, Mellon, Rockefeller, and the American Council of Learned Societies, which grants funds provided by other sources) expand the number of fellowships available to humanists.

In our discussion of graduate training in the humanities, we noted the shortage of tenurable academic posts for Ph.D.'s. Against the day when this condition eases, it is essential to maintain the careers of younger humanists who represent the future of teaching and scholarship in their fields. The best of these will need the opportunity to earn a livelihood, whether through teaching or in a nonacademic setting, and support for the development of their potential as scholars. Fellowship agencies should provide support for scholarship to humanists *at various stages* of their careers, from postdoctoral to senior.

The NEH's Division of Fellowships has started to give special attention to applications from humanists at two-year and smaller four-year institutions and from young scholars at major universities. Among private foundations, the Andrew W. Mellon Foundation has liberally supported younger humanists. Between 1974 and 1976, the foundation provided $22 million to various universities for over three hundred postdoctoral appointments. The foundation has also supported humanists at mid-career, granting $9.3 million on a matching basis in 1978 and nearly $5 million in 1979 to a number of major universities "to enable them to create opportunities for appointing, retaining, or advancing to tenure some outstanding younger talent where this would not otherwise be possible." In 1978 Mellon also awarded $1 million to the American Council of Learned Societies in support of a fellowship program for young Ph.D.'s (*Report of the Andrew W. Mellon Foundation, 1978,* New York).

For sixty years the American Council of Learned Societies has provided services to scholars in the humanities. Its programs of support, though not on a grand scale, are exemplary in their distribution of resources among various levels of scholarship; in

1978, for instance, the Council awarded 70 postdoctoral fellow-ships to scholars at different stages of their careers, 31 fellowships to recent recipients of the Ph.D., 171 grants-in-aid of the research projects of established and younger scholars, 143 travel grants, and 22 awards to senior graduate students. Now the future financial stability—indeed the very existence—of the ACLS is imperiled. The ACLS is a regrant agency, and funds to support its central programs will be exhausted after June 1982. To insure long-term financial security, the ACLS has undertaken a Sixtieth Anniversary Campaign to gain sufficient endowment and program funds to continue its activities at their present level. It is seeking support from major foundations, leading business corporations, and the federal government, and is asking for a federal charter to the ACLS as the private organization, analogous to the National Academy of Sciences, symbolizing our nation's concern for the humanities. We believe it is in the national interest that the ACLS receive both the federal charter and the necessary financial support, for its role in relation to humanistic scholarship is essential.

Scholarship in the humanities is vital to the nation. It seldom leads straight to widely visible results. In times of retrenchment and increased accountability, this fact is perhaps the humanities' misfortune. It is also their virtue. Scholarship should never be the handmaiden of public policy or public whim. Society must be the subject of scholarship, not its master; its finest insights are often achieved in quite private regions of specialized study long before they can reach a wide audience.

From its inception, a major purpose of the NEH has been "the development and dissemination of knowledge of the humanities through research and other scholarly activities in order to increase our national resources in the humanities" (*First Annual Report,* Washington, D.C., 1966). The Endowment's allocations for scholarship have remained substantial as the agency has developed its other missions, especially its mandate to acquaint the general public with the humanities. In connection with this mandate, the NEH has regularly emphasized scholarly projects with a special "relevance to important problems of the day" (*Third Annual Report,* 1968) or studies "that appeal to the imaginations of

Americans in general" (*Thirteenth Annual Report*, 1978). Some private fellowship programs have posted similar guidelines for their awards. Since 1973, moreover, the Endowment's Division of Fellowships has allocated considerable sums for fellowships and seminars for the professions—journalism, medicine, and the like.

We have argued throughout this report that the humanities must be more accessible to the public, and we have urged humanists to explore the avenues open to them for "going public." But we are concerned about a possible overemphasis on tailoring humanistic scholarship for relevance to contemporary issues or for immediate accessibility. Research is as important in the humanities as in the sciences; often it cannot be applied, and indeed it often reveals applications never before dreamed of. Scholars in the humanities continually reinterpret our world, whether the subject be the energy crisis or the Peloponnesian Wars. The results of their work filter into society through classes in schools and colleges, through reviews and articles in the popular press, through the reading of individuals and discussions among friends. The relevance and vigor of the humanities can be maintained only by nurturing research and scholarship in a manner free from constraint.

Historically, being a professional humanist has meant being a teacher and a scholar. But the face of the profession is changing. The shortage of academic jobs has driven many individuals with advanced training and scholarly ambitions into careers outside educational institutions and beyond easy access to libraries, professional colleagues, and students. Yet these individuals, too, are humanists, trained for scholarship and capable of contributing to their fields.

Independent institutes and research organizations have sprung up, expressions of the scholarly interests of nonacademic humanists. New York's Institute for Research in History, for example, encourages research through workshops, symposia, and the like. Its members, some of whom have published in scholarly journals, include academic and nonacademic historians.

Learned societies are fast becoming professional associations, and we recognize that some of our suggestions may accelerate this evolution. Traditionally dedicated to the advancement of scholarship, they now also help young scholars find jobs, raise funds, sponsor programs on teaching in high schools and community colleges and on the needs of ethnic minorities, and so on. These functions bring learned societies into political and social realms that, to some of their members, seem to be the antithesis of scholarship. Other members, however, would argue that the learned societies have not yet adequately discharged the responsibilities imposed on them by their role as guardians of humanistic learning and by their pleas for public support. A number of humanists, believing that the humanities need a general membership association, established in 1978 the American Association for the Advancement of the Humanities. It emphasizes the need for more effective advocacy and outreach by humanists, in education and in the community, and it has close ties with another fledgling group, the Community College Humanities Association.

New modes of sharing scholarly knowledge, the changing fortunes of higher education, the many new roles imposed on humanists by the "learning society": these promise to stretch the meaning of the word *humanist* and change the profession. Regulating the pace of that change, making it work for the benefit of education and scholarship in the humanities, will be up to individual humanists, educational and cultural institutions, and the learned societies. Their first duty—to preserve the integrity of learning in the humanities—will need a fine touch for the possibilities and limits of innovation. Their most noble aspiration should be to bring the past to life today and pass it on to tomorrow.

The experience of the last three decades has clearly shown that the fortunes of the humanities, higher education, and our culture are closely interwoven. The prosperity in higher education in the 1950s and 1960s, itself a reflection of our nation's material and technical progress, was in some respects a boon for the humanities. The economic stringencies and social reappraisals of the 1970s, and the consequent reassessments of higher education, will inevitably continue to test the strength of the humanities. Administrators and legislators, humanists, students, and the public must share responsibility for preserving and channeling that strength. All must reaffirm that the equation linking our culture with higher education and the humanities runs in both directions: the humanities are a part of what we need to know about ourselves and a broad avenue to discovering the uses of that knowledge.

CHAPTER FOUR 🌿

The Humanities
in Community
and Private Life

The interests and aspirations of many people turn naturally toward
the humanities through concern for freedom, moral values, beauty,
and knowledge of the past. Yet in the public mind the term
humanities often suggests remote intellectual activity or narrow
academic professionalism. One of our national objectives should be
to resolve this seeming paradox. As we cope with the urgent rush
of day-to-day affairs, from controversies over nuclear energy to
frustration at the myriad difficulties of our individual lives, we
must argue for the active role of the humanities in shaping this
country's future. We must stress how limited our sense of national
purpose is, indeed how imperiled our civilization is, if the
humanities are exiled to a peripheral role of irrelevance.

The increasing use of the modes of education discussed in this
chapter show that education is not an occasional, abrupt event, nor
a series of episodes we experience from September to June when
we are between the ages of five and twenty-one. Education is a
constant shaping, sometimes as deliberate and structured as
sculpture, sometimes haphazard and unnoticed, like the wear on
stone steps. The humanities are specific courses, disciplines, or
works identified in the curricula of schools and colleges; but they
are also implicit in our everyday lives—in the critical standards of
judgment we use when we prefer one book or movie to another or

when we say "nice work" or "good idea," and in questions about how we want to live and what tasks we undertake. How and why do we act differently from generations before us? Are particular cultural forms and political issues of our era unprecedented? Shall we interpret the phrases *quality of life* and *leisure time* in a material or a spiritual sense? Does freedom mean one thing for racial minorities and another for suburban whites? Why do feminists put so much emphasis on the word *person?*

Our different needs and customs lead us to the humanities for different reasons. Some people look especially for private self-enrichment, others for ways to apply their ideas to community life. Some want to share experiences between parents and children, others with people of the same generation or those going through a similar stage of reevaluation. Some of us search for new cultural works or creative outlets, others find pleasure in perceiving old works through new lenses. Some prefer traditional forms of the Western cultural heritage, others the expression of racial, ethnic, regional, or non-Western cultures.

We can only *begin* to measure public interest in the humanities by counting the people who enroll in adult education courses, attend museums and lectures, use libraries, watch "Roots" or "Great Performances" on television, or respond in certain ways to national polls. For registrars and turnstiles cannot measure how, as the Russian poet Osip Mandelstam wrote in 1922, "every family clings to its own intonations, its personal references, and to its own special meanings of words defined in parentheses" (*Mandelstam: The Complete Prose and Letters,* ed. Jane G. Harris, Ann Arbor, 1979). Whether the special meanings of words and images belong to individuals, families, or communities, they touch the humanities in ways that often defy precise definition. Thus any attempt to classify humanistic pursuits beyond the normal routines of schools and colleges must be somewhat artificial. In this chapter we have proceeded according to types of institutions, partly for convenience but chiefly because we believe that broadened public learning in the humanities may best be achieved by appealing through our established educational and cultural institutions to diverse public interests.

Other models for describing public learning in the humanities include at least one that cuts across institutions: the audiences that participate in such activities. Various groups define and enjoy the humanities according to their own lights. But we would warn against too great an emphasis on specific constituencies, lest it result in a disregard for the integrity of the institutions housing America's cultural resources. There are parallel risks in narrow institutional self-interest, which is antithetical to the creative public reevaluation of tradition that is part of the humanities. Institutions must preserve our heritage in the humanities, but they must also provide access to and interpretation of that heritage. In ways consistent with their missions, institutions such as community colleges, museums, and libraries must and often do encourage public participation in their decisions. Neither institutions nor the public should lose sight of the humanities' capacity for enriching individual lives through essentially private acts of contemplation and creation—private even when the subject is a public issue and the purpose active citizenship.

Although we have organized this chapter according to categories of institutions, then, we would argue that strengthening the humanities in community and private life requires these delicate balances: between the preservative and interpretive functions of our educational and cultural institutions; between the humanities as a set of traditions and as a body of living lore that evolves through public participation; and between the private enrichment and public responsibility of individuals.

Maintaining these balances involves particular obligations. Academic humanists, accustomed to seeing themselves as specialists and cultural custodians, can more frequently participate in appropriate forms of nontraditional learning—in extension courses, for example, or in programs sponsored by the State Humanities Committees affiliated with the National Endowment for the Humanities (NEH). They must also be prepared to speak out as citizens on issues of civic consequence or explain their scholarly work to larger public audiences.

Although the adult members of these audiences often see a closer connection between learning and living than do students in schools and colleges, many view the humanities as irrelevant to real life. Others expect the humanities to provide clear-cut answers to all questions of value. Between these extremes, adult learners should look to the humanities for invaluable assistance in enriching cultural memory and individual experience, sharpening critical faculties, and increasing awareness of the less visible costs and advantages of public policies.

Educational institutions must resist the temptation to respond to financially hard times by cutting back programs in the humanities merely because they bring in less income than vocational courses. Equally unfortunate would be the reduction of the humanities to a pabulum of instant gratification or immediate relevance to appeal to a large clientele. Educational administrators must encourage their faculties to interrelate academic and public conceptions of the humanities. Administrators must also seek ways to increase the community's understanding of the humanistic activity inside and outside the walls of their institutions.

Schools and colleges, museums, libraries, historical organizations, and the noncommercial media must collaborate to serve the public. Federal and state governments, private foundations, corporations, and individuals should regard nontraditional learning in the humanities as a sound social investment. They should be prepared to sponsor both bold innovations and established programs, projects for special groups (racial, ethnic, occupational, and so on) as well as exhibits that draw large crowds. Sources of support should remain willing to accept the risk involved in funding innovative projects or programs of limited appeal, but should not give so disproportionately to the faddish or experimental—a particular danger in a culture preoccupied with novelty—that traditional programs are neglected. Foundations and federal agencies often prefer to seed new projects rather than sustain old ones; they are reluctant to subsidize operating costs that include the preservation of materials in museums, libraries, and other places. That millions of books and magazines are disintegrating is an ecological fact of enormous public consequence. Preservation—and the training in skills it requires—may indeed be the most important and least risky investment the federal government can make in our national culture.

The obligation shared by all is to promote public access to institutions and activities where learning in the humanities takes place. In this chapter we describe promising programs in the humanities that have come to our attention and suggest ways to strengthen the humanities in community and private life. Since we have not provided an exhaustive inventory of the humanities in our culture, we ought here to mention a few areas we consider no less important than those described at greater length below.

We join with the Commission on the Humanities of 1964 in regarding the visual and performing arts as intimately related to the humanities and essential to their existence (*Report of the Commission on the Humanities,* New York, 1964). From the beginnings of culture, the arts have expressed humanistic values; for centuries the humanities have reflected on artistic creation, exploring the interplay of form, method, and idea that art represents. The phenomenal growth of public interest in the arts over the past fifteen years betokens a deepening American appreciation for creative expressions of the human spirit. Each year, more Americans attend exhibitions of the visual arts and presentations of the performing arts than attend spectator sports. Modern dance and ballet attracted over fifteen million people in 1977, as opposed to less than one million a decade earlier. Attendance at opera increased fivefold between 1950 and 1978, and the number of opera companies has jumped from a pre-Second World War level of seventy-seven to over nine hundred today. There are now well over three hundred professional theater companies, compared to a meager two dozen ten years ago. Nearly fourteen hundred symphony orchestras draw listeners from communities across the land. Television has brought musical and theatrical performances of high caliber into the homes of millions of viewers.

Together with the National Endowment for the Arts (NEA), sister agency to the NEH, hundreds of state and community arts organizations, corporations, foundations, and other groups have nurtured the growth of the arts in America. Unable to recover their costs at the box office, the arts have always depended on society's patronage and probably always will. While a thorough examination of the arts is beyond our purview, we must assert that sustained support for the arts in America is fundamental to the vitality of the humanities. Our society's enthusiasm for the arts is a measure of its interest in the humanities and an opportunity for advancing that interest.

Surprising as it may seem, research libraries can and often do connect the humanities with public life. Traditionally, university and independent research libraries have been conservators of records of the past, and they have served scholars and advanced students in the humanities. Now an increasing number of research libraries—notably independent research libraries such as the Folger, Huntington, Morgan, and Newberry—also include public programs among their activities. "Going public" is not easy for most research libraries. Not every library should be expected to have this mission, nor can each discharge it as easily as another, for the chief functions of research libraries are still the conservation and scholarly use of valuable records of the past. But in the past few decades, having recognized that their traditional base of support is limited, research libraries have accepted an obligation to increase access to their collections in return for public financial support. They are reaching out to larger audiences through programs for schools and colleges, noncredit seminars, interpretive exhibits (including some traveling exhibits), lectures, and popular publications, and in fields such as community history, poetry, cartography, and genealogy. In short, research libraries are becoming centers for using research in nontraditional learning.

Most centers of advanced study do not share the custodial mission or public accessibility of the cultural institutions discussed below. Not every institute can add public outreach to its central mission of scholarly study. Still, some institutes—such as the Aspen Institute for Humanistic Studies, the Hastings Center, the National Humanities Center, the Woodrow Wilson International Center for Scholars, the University of Maryland Center for Philosophy and Public Policy, the University of Southern California Center for the Humanities, the Institute for Humanistic Studies at the State University of New York, Albany, and the New York Institute for the Humanities, New York University— consciously serve as brokers between scholarship and the public through conferences, lectures, publications, and collaboration with other cultural and educational institutions. Whether they are independent or attached to universities, institutes can overcome compartmentalization by bringing together scholars, artists, educators, and representatives from business, labor, politics, and other sectors. They can deal with issues of public consequence more easily than many universities seem able to, especially issues that require cross-disciplinary approaches: ethical questions in the professions, politics, and science; the benefits and dangers of technology. On these and other urgent concerns, institutes can heighten public awareness of the historical, ethical, and aesthetic perspectives afforded by scholarship in the humanities.

Countless voluntary associations study the humanities, from reading clubs to groups of scholars working outside the walls of universities. Religious institutions and community organizations with a religious orientation are probably the most active in this regard. Religious education is of course an important part of churches' and synagogues' service to their congregations, and the place of religion in education and community life is a topic of many local and national programs of the major faiths.

Of the many other groups whose activities touch on the humanities we can note only a few. The Great Books reading and discussion groups number over fifty thousand members in twenty-five hundred groups nationwide, and the Great Books Foundation of Chicago provides low-cost paperback texts and two-day workshops for group leaders. The American Association of Retired Persons sponsors discussion groups on topics from physics to philosophy, with reading materials published in its magazine, *Modern Maturity*. Recalling an earlier era, the Chautauqua Literary and Scientific Circle, once a circuit of nine thousand communities but now limited to a single site in New York State, enjoys a resurgence of public interest in its lectures on literary, philosophical, and political topics. The Center for the Book, created in the Library of Congress in 1977, works with other organizations concerned with education and publishing to stimulate appreciation for books and encourage reading; in a project called Read More About It, for example, the Center has offered viewers information about books related to special programs on a major television network.

State Humanities Committees (or Councils), which receive funds from the NEH and other sources, frequently support programs sponsored by local groups and voluntary associations. Until 1976 the State Committees were required by Congress to emphasize issues of public policy in their granting activities, and many states focused on audiences traditionally excluded from learning in the humanities. Several recent programs sponsored by the State Committees reflect a combination of these purposes: forums on "Jobs for Chicanos" given by the Labor Council for Latin American Advancement (Washington); a lecture series for prison inmates called "Women and Violence," coordinated by Art Without Walls/Free Space, an arts group in New York; and the Sussex Pomona Grange's program on the effects of social and technological change on traditional farmers and their way of life (Delaware). The emphasis on public policy has also led to several programs for business and community leaders, labor unions, and professional groups.

Since the State Committees were allowed to establish their own guidelines and priorities, considerable diversity has characterized the projects they support and the groups applying for grants. Community forums remain a popular format for state-sponsored programs. By and large, the State Committees provide vital support—indeed sometimes the only support—for public activities in the humanities, and they are in an advantageous position to help coordinate the work of educational and cultural institutions.

EDUCATIONAL INSTITUTIONS

Over the past decade, adult enrollments in educational institutions have greatly expanded. The number of colleges and universities offering adult education more than doubled from 1,102 in 1967–68 to 2,225 in 1977–78, and enrollments increased from 5.6 million to 8.8 million. Public school systems have carried on their tradition of providing educational services to adults. Various organizations have joined the movement to offer educational services to adult or nontraditional learners. Informational networks and counseling centers help match adult learners with local educational resources. Reports by the Carnegie Commission on Higher Education and the Commission on Non-Traditional Study, the Lifelong Learning Act of 1976, and the College Board's current program, Future Directions for a Learning Society, have all emphasized the many opportunities in continuing education. These and other studies give little attention to the humanities, but reports from the National University Extension Association (NUEA) and the American Association of Community and Junior Colleges indicate increasing interest in workshops, community forums, and noncredit courses in the humanities. Many adults who return to institutions of higher learning do so in search of humanistic values that seem to have been left out of their formal education.

In general, educators lack reliable data on how many courses in continuing education include the humanities, and what these courses offer the learner—in part because the categories by which courses are usually classified (vocational or career education, hobbies and recreation, general education, home and family life, personal development, and the like) obscure such information. Still, there is clear evidence of opportunities for adding the humanities to adult education and of innovative efforts to do so.

Vocational Education

Approximately half of all programs of adult and continuing education are occupational, yet vocational schools and the educational programs of labor and industry rarely include courses in the humanities. Industry, for example, employs over forty-five thousand teachers and spends over $4 billion annually to improve efficiency and productivity through training programs for workers. Many programs in industrial education have added basic or remedial education as companies recognize the importance of basic skills in most jobs. Courses in the humanities, however, are limited to managers and executives. Likewise, most university programs for workers focus on the technical requirements of industrial labor, seldom including the humanities or other liberal studies.

Much of the growth in occupational education has occurred in community colleges. Between 1970 and 1976 the number of occupational degrees conferred by these institutions doubled; it is estimated that more than half of all community college students are currently enrolled in occupational programs. The training acquired by these occupational students represents a sort of educational paradox. For many, the need to develop skills for immediate entry into the job market overshadows the idea of general education; the certification requirements of state accrediting agencies and of trades advisory councils reinforce this way of thinking. Consequently, the growth in vocational enrollments has been accompanied by a decline in enrollments in the humanities and in the reading and writing skills of occupational graduates—skills needed both on the job and off.

Study of the humanities is neither possible nor appropriate in all areas of vocational education—for example, in vocational schools providing short-term training for specific technical occupations. Nevertheless, with post-secondary vocational enrollments up from 144,000 in 1963 to well over two million in 1979, it is important to recognize that the humanities help develop the capacities for communication and decision making in technical careers and enrich people's lives beyond their jobs.

RECOMMENDATION 16:   Humanists and occupational educators together should develop curricula in the humanities for programs of technical and vocational education; administrators should encourage the use of resources in the humanities—including the active participation of humanists—for occupational programs.

As we observed in the preceding chapter on higher education, vocational students can be introduced to humanistic studies if these are imaginatively integrated with occupational training. The experience of many community colleges and four-year institutions has shown the importance of collaboration between faculty in the humanities and in occupational fields. Yet many humanists show little interest in developing curricula that make use of the relationships among their own disciplines and vocations. They must be challenged to explore how the content of their disciplines can be enriched, rather than cheapened or distorted, by presenting it in ways that interest vocational students.

Institutional and program administrators must take an active, well-articulated interest in these endeavors. In a recent study of two-year institutions, the Center for the Study of Community Colleges found that where the humanities thrive they do so with the help of administrators who frequently state their belief in the importance of the humanities, aid their faculty and staff in obtaining funds for innovative programs, and actively enlist student and community interest in these courses (*The Humanities in Two-Year Colleges: Trends in Curriculum,* Los Angeles, 1978). We join the Center, the Community College Humanities Association, and the assembly convened in November 1979 by the American Association of Community and Junior Colleges in recommending that community colleges (and, we would add, other institutions offering technical and vocational training) organize interested members of the local community into lay advisory committees to help integrate the humanities with career education. These groups should include representatives from the trades advisory councils and other agencies that establish requirements for vocational education. As role models, placement advisors, and recruiting agents, the members of these advisory committees can act as advocates for the humanities among occupational students and in the community.

Adult Basic Education

Large federally funded programs in Adult Basic Education (ABE), currently enrolling two to four million learners, stress skills in reading, writing, and computation at elementary levels. Standardized tests and measurable objectives often determine the content of classes where drill, recitation, and workbook assignments are the norm. One widely used program, developed through federally funded research at a major university, lists dozens of learning objectives for the illiterate adult, but virtually excludes imagination, creativity, or reflection on one's place in the world.

RECOMMENDATION 17: Programs of basic education or skill development for adults should use materials from the humanities that actively involve participants and broaden their learning.

Materials that draw on the humanities can bring ABE learners to a better understanding of themselves and issues concerning them. Some groups have developed such materials. The Literacy Volunteers of America, Inc., has compiled a *Bibliography of Humanistic Readings for Grade Levels 1–8* (Syracuse, 1979) for use in ABE programs and public library tutorial centers. This organization urges teachers to let adult learners select readings of special interest and create their own study materials.

• In a St. Paul, Virginia, school, an ABE class of long-time residents of a mining community created a photographic history of life in the coal mines. The El Barrio project in San Antonio, Texas, began in 1975 with a focus on health care for a group of expectant mothers and expanded to include art and music as components of a literacy-in-Spanish program.

Continuing Education

Traditional offerings in the humanities in university extension and continuing education divisions, two-year colleges, and public school adult education are not expanding; many, in fact, are declining. One authority in the field observes, "The average adult learner does not regard traditional liberal arts courses as the foundation subjects that will satisfy his or her need for new knowledge. Only small minorities of adults express a strong interest in traditional discipline-based subjects, and these learners, predictably, are those with high levels of educational attainment" (Patricia Cross, "Adult Learners: Characteristics, Needs, and Interests," in R. E. Peterson et al., *Lifelong Learning in America*, San Francisco, 1979). Adult educators find that continuing education programs in the humanities, as in other fields, must be tailored to the particular interests of adult learners.

RECOMMENDATION 18: College and university faculty in the humanities, faculty in adult and continuing education, and the staffs of cultural and community institutions should cooperate in the development of humanistic programs for adults in order to pool resources, identify the needs and interests of adult audiences, and ensure high quality.

Universities and colleges should not segregate continuing education from higher education as if the former were not the responsibility of the regular faculty. Humanities and extension departments have valuable counsel to offer each other.

As described by Milton Stern, Dean of University Extension at the University of California, Berkeley, "The adult student, not pursuing a degree—and most of them do not—is eclectic in the humanities, interested more or less deeply in specific aspects of a subject, and in limited sequences of courses" (Address to the NEH-NUEA Conference on Continuing Education in the Humanities, Memphis, 14 February 1979). Thus successful courses in the humanities frequently focus on a specific theme or topic, often drawing on several academic disciplines. Some programs expand or new courses arise in order to tie in with current issues or events, such as museum exhibits, energy, conservation, or inflation. Courses offered by individual institutions involve faculty from several departments and use community resources such as museums and libraries. Many programs depend on collaboration among several educational institutions, often using electronic media to reach widespread publics.

• The Bard College Center of Bard College, a private liberal arts institution in Annandale-on-Hudson, New York, mobilizes the resources of the college and the community in order to "improve the quality and availability of educational and cultural resources for citizens of all ages in the Hudson Valley region; and to promote the study and the use of the liberal arts in public planning and decision-making processes that will affect the quality of life in the Hudson Valley and other regions" (*First Annual Report, 1978–1979,* Annandale-on-Hudson). The Center sponsors lectures and seminars given by distinguished fellows from government, business, the arts, education, and public life; conferences and community forums; intensive weekend and summer programs; and exhibits and performances in the arts.

• Another example of a partnership between an institution of higher education and surrounding cultural institutions is the Capital District Humanities Program now being developed by the College of Humanities and Fine Arts at the State University of New York, Albany. The major goals of this project are to make the adult program a regular part of academic life at the university, provide staff development through an internship program, and establish a resource center on adult education in the humanities for national use. External sources supporting the program include the NEH, the New York Council for the Humanities, state agencies, foundations, and individuals.

• The University of Georgia's Center for Continuing Education reaches a statewide audience through the collaboration of several institutions. University faculty from the humanities and related disciplines develop materials for use by other colleges and universities, local study groups, and individuals. In a program called "Land Use," for example, a monograph prepared by university faculty from philosophy, law, natural resources, and environmental design provided the background for discussions; the Georgia Committee for the Humanities helped fund this program.

• The University of Mid-America (UMA, based at the University of Nebraska), a consortium of eleven universities in seven states, delivers college-level courses to off-campus students through television and other media. Over ten thousand students have registered for credit at member institutions; many have enrolled without credit as well. UMA exports courses for use at nonmember institutions and these have now reached a total audience of eight hundred thousand. Supported in part by a large grant from the National Institute of Education, UMA has developed twelve courses, including some in the humanities. UMA is now developing shorter course "modules" in order to appeal to a larger noncredit audience and is collaborating with local libraries, historical societies, and museums.

Many institutions have designed programs for special populations with common interests, including professionals, executives and managers, workers, families, the elderly, and prisoners. Through their continuing education divisions and alumni associations, many colleges and universities sponsor on-campus classes, special workshops, and "colleges" for alumni, their families and friends, and increasingly for the public at large. A recent guidebook, *Learning Vacations*, lists over four hundred such programs. By working with community agencies and service organizations, some institutions have reached adults with little prior education. Through "weekend colleges" and classes in the community or workplace, institutions accommodate the working schedules of particular groups while making greater use of institutional resources.

• Elderhostel, an on-campus summer program, offers liberal arts studies to people over sixty, until recently one of the most neglected groups in adult education. Started in 1975 at five institutions, the program seeks "to serve older adults by responding to their capacity to meet change and intellectual challenge and by nourishing in them a spirit of adventure" (*Elderhostel Annual Report 1978*, Newton, Mass.). In 1979 some thirteen thousand people participated in the program on 233 college campuses in thirty-eight states. By 1983 program administrators hope to be serving about sixty thousand participants at over 400 institutions. Foundations and corporations have supported the development of the program, but by 1983 Elderhostel hopes to support itself through tuition charges.

• The School of New Resources of the College of New Rochelle has a liberal arts degree program for adults who have not had the opportunity for higher education. Begun under the leadership of the former chairman of the college's Department of Philosophy, the program has spread to several locations. The campus in New Rochelle serves economically and racially diverse suburban residents. A program designed especially for the munici-pal employees in the local unions of District Council 37 of New York City is situated on union premises. Other programs serve residents of a large housing project, Black and Hispanic residents of the South Bronx, and church workers and storefront ministers. In all of these, students participate in developing a liberal arts curriculum meeting their own needs for self-understanding and critical skills.

• Although newspapers, radio, and television have helped open opportunities to people who cannot attend educational institutions, it has been especially difficult to interest rural populations in programs in the humanities. By cooperating with the university's Agricultural Extension Service, the North Carolina State Humanities Extension has begun to overcome obstacles in rural areas. County agents enlist influential community members to identify local interests and serve as discussion leaders in seminars on appropriate humanistic themes. The seminars use materials prepared by regular university faculty, who also participate in a few group discussions. To expand faculty contact with distant groups, the Extension Service plans to try telephone hookups and cable television.

If continuing education in the humanities is to thrive, educational institutions must continually identify the interests of adult learners and energetically promote new courses. The marketing of continuing education raises fears among humanists that popularizing the humanities will cheapen and vulgarize them. These fears are not groundless. Yet we believe that broadening public participation in the humanities is not only in the interest of the humanities, but in the public interest as well; and we urge humanists to be more active in reaching public audiences. It is possible to mediate between the academic disciplines of the humanities and the humanistic interests of the public in a zone where the humanities and the public both benefit. Not every increase in the sheer numbers of people participating in programs labeled *humanities* is necessarily a real gain. We endorse the popularization of the humanities, but only through programs of real quality and depth.

Particularly in state universities, state colleges, and community colleges, which are in a unique position to bring academic and public pursuits together, programs of faculty development are needed. The aim of many current programs is to enrich the experience of faculty as well as that of adult learners. Outreach from college and university humanists need not merely respond to public demand; it can also show the community what goes on within these institutions and thus increase understanding of traditional forms of humanistic learning.

Financial support for adult and continuing education in the humanities is lean. Private foundations (the W. K. Kellogg Foundation is noteworthy), the National Endowment for the Humanities, State Humanities Committees, and other donors have contributed to faculty and program development in the humanities. Continued support will be necessary from these sources and from the governing boards of public and private educational institutions. Some of the most promising strategies for extending the humanities to greater numbers of nontraditional learners—such as the use of communications media, or the collaboration of educational institutions and community service organizations—require considerable cooperation and cost sharing among institutions and funding sources. In a period of tightened budgets and competing priorities, state and local governments must not neglect the humanities; nor should they view federal or private support as an excuse to diminish their own efforts on behalf of the humanities.

CULTURAL INSTITUTIONS

In the institutions discussed below, public learning in the humanities takes place—or depends upon resources from—inside walls that were not built to house curricular and administrative mechanisms for granting degrees. There are of course important differences among these institutions and the ways the public uses them. People are more likely to go in groups or as families to museums than to libraries. Museums of history and science are noisier and have more moving parts than art museums. Public libraries have fewer scholars and more children per square foot than do research libraries. The use of public libraries and museums cuts across social groups and generations, and most of us remember our first museum visit or library card as an important initiation (and it was). Whatever their differences, however, these institutions combine custodial and educational missions in the interest of our national culture, and they mediate in various ways between educational institutions and the public. Because they do not grant degrees, they can be more flexible and more accessible than most formal educational institutions. For the same reason, however, their educational value is easy to underestimate, and public support for them is likely to slip in times of inflation and retrenchment. Cultural institutions and continuing education must nurture each other, or both will wither.

Government agencies, other sources of support, and the public should recognize the importance of the preservative functions that increase the operating expenses of major cultural institutions. Many of the books, paintings, documents, and artifacts housed by museums, libraries, and historical organizations may not interest large public audiences. Nevertheless, our heritage in the humanities is a national treasure and its preservation a public trust.

We emphasize the need for a general assessment of national policy and mechanisms for cultural preservation. Unlike some other nations, this country lacks a broad legislative or administrative definition of cultural heritage and preservation. In Japan, for example, the Law for the Preservation of Cultural Properties designates various kinds of tangible and intangible treasures, including individuals trained in certain ancient skills (such as the maker of articles for a Buddhist altar). By contrast, the criteria generally used by Congress, the Department of the Interior's Heritage Conservation and Recreation Service, the Advisory Council on Historic Preservation, the National Trust for Historic Preservation, and other offices focus on tangible property and seldom delve into questions of cultural or human value.

In 1977 a federal task force attempted to reassess national policy by considering the full range of the nation's cultural and recreational resources. They made some progress, in spite of disagreements over guidelines and priorities. The agencies mentioned above, together with the National Park Service and other public and private groups, continue to reassess their policies, and legislation has been proposed concerning historical and cultural preservation. We urge that any assessment or legislation take a broad view of culture and define the humanities as a national cultural interest. Criteria for designating properties to be preserved should include their social and aesthetic contexts (the Swedish Central Office of National Antiquities gives this emphasis to preservation), and policies for cultural preservation should recognize the importance of unique skills. Policies must distinguish among kinds of cultural institutions and the resources held by them—books, manuscripts, paintings, sculpture, artifacts, costumes, recordings and films of the performing arts, and so forth—and must also consider the kinds and numbers of users of these resources: public support obliges institutions to give unrestrained access to those people who can make use of their materials. Federal policies should promote cooperation among cultural institutions, recognize the relationship between preservation and interpretive programs, and insure regular public funding of operating expenses of cultural institutions through renewable, long-term matching support and through project grants that do not rigidly distinguish between programs and operations. Finally, ways must be found to reduce confusion among government agencies and to foster collaboration among them in the pursuit of national cultural goals, with due regard for the perspectives of the two National Endowments.

Museums

Public interest in museums has increased over the past fifteen years when measured by attendance, membership, volunteer staff participation, services, and the number of museums in existence. Over 750 new museums have been founded since 1969 alone. Speaking on the idea of a White House Conference on the Humanities (proposed for 1978 or 1979 but never held), E. Leland Webber, president of the Field Museum of Natural History in Chicago, referred to the large cross-section of American citizens served by museums:

A large metropolitan museum today serves people in age from preschool to senior citizen, in educational level from elementary to postdoctoral, in duration from an hour to a lifetime, in location from an exhibit hall to a library and even to distant parts of the earth, in formality from completely solitary and self-directed to lectures, courses, and supervised predoctoral research, and in purpose from recreational to vocational. (*Joint Hearings Before Subcommittees of the House Committee on Education and Labor and the Senate Committee on Human Resources*, 13 January 1978)

In 1978 museums counted nearly 360 million visitors, or about six times the number of spectators at all professional baseball, football, and basketball games.

Many museum directors identify education as the most important mission of their institutions, recognizing that our cultural heritage should not be kept in storage but should be understood and enjoyed. Museums are uniquely capable of demonstrating the complexity of culture in a manner appealing to the senses as well as the intellect. Interpretive exhibits can provide visitors with historical, social, aesthetic, technological, and ethnic contexts for contemplating objects. Without such information, understanding and enjoying cultural artifacts are severely restricted.

RECOMMENDATION 19: Museums should mount more exhibits informing visitors of the cultural, aesthetic, historical, and technical forces surrounding the creation of the objects displayed. More use of permanent collections and more sharing of collections among institutions would increase public access to our national treasury of historical and cultural artifacts.

The resources of museums can enhance educational programs in the humanities. As many exhibits prove, education, entertainment, and social interaction are mutually inclusive. In some art museums, visitors paint and sculpt with materials provided, but an active response to works of art or other displays need not (and often simply cannot) depend on a literal "hands-on" approach. The success of many exhibits derives in part from the social nature of the museum experience, according to researchers at the Lawrence Hall of Science: generally, people attend museums (especially those of history, science, technology, and natural history) as families, friends, or in groups, and view museums as a social environment for learning.

Programs for schoolchildren form the largest category of educational activities sponsored by museums. These programs vary in frequency from an annual field trip to a series of six monthly visits, in method from lectures to treasure hunts. While museum programs should not replace a strong curriculum in the arts or other subjects, they provide learning opportunities unmatched by ordinary school resources. However, museums' educational programs generally serve high school students less well than they do younger students. With more assistance from federal, state, and private sources of support, museums can fill gaps in the school curriculum and make special efforts to reach students of high school age.

The two National Endowments, State Humanities Committees, and other public and private sponsors have helped museums stimulate community interest by drawing attention to the cultural contributions of racial and ethnic minorities. Community arts projects—many of them supported by the NEA, municipal agencies, and private foundations—increase the participation of neighborhood residents. Some museums also send parts of their collections into the community through neighborhood branches and mobile exhibits. With encouragement from the NEH and State Humanities Committees, museums of local history have fostered public awareness of community history. Museums of science and natural history have strengthened their ties with the humanities, thanks especially to the efforts of the NEH, which is the main (but by no means adequate) source of support for humanistic approaches to scientific exhibits. We hope that the National Science Foundation will be able to offer more support than it has given in past years to humanistic programs in museums of science and technology.

• In *The Art Museum as Educator* (Berkeley and Los Angeles, 1978), the Council on Museums and Education in the Visual Arts has compiled an extensive collection of exemplary museum activities. Some of the programs tested visitors in creative ways in order to heighten their critical appreciation of the visual arts; for example, "Fakes, Forgeries, and Other Deceptions" at the Minneapolis Institute of Arts juxtaposed authentic works with imitations of high quality and challenged visitors to distinguish between them. Among the programs for schoolchildren cited, some—such as the East Cleveland Project, which emphasized the relationship between the visual arts and verbal skills—resulted in measurable improvement in students' overall academic achievement.

• The NEH has supported several museum projects focusing on state and local history—for example, a set of permanent displays at the museum of Northern Arizona in Flagstaff telling the story of the Native American peoples of the Colorado plateau; and a temporary exhibit at the North Carolina Museum of History tracing the history of Black North Carolinians from their African origins to the end of the nineteenth century.

• The Smithsonian Institution's programs exemplify a number of services that museums can offer. Its Traveling Exhibition Service circulates exhibits to hundreds of cities. The Studies Seminar program in Washington, D.C., combines illustrated lectures with tours behind the scenes. The Study Tour program provides expert guidance through the museum's many facilities for domestic and foreign travelers.

Recent "blockbuster" exhibits, among the most visible signs of increased public interest in the arts, have been controversial as well as popular. Some museum personnel welcome the public interest in such shows as the Treasures of Tutankhamen and the Splendor of Dresden. They cite the increases in museum attendance and membership that follow large temporary exhibits. Other museum officials, however, argue that these increases quickly subside and that large exhibits deflect precious resources from the care and display of permanent collections. Simply standing before treasured works of art confers no special knowledge on any individual. Large temporary exhibits should introduce visitors to the historical and cultural contexts of the works on display and should draw viewers to a museum's permanent collection. Some museums have done so by spotlighting those parts of their collection relating to the subject of a traveling exhibit, or by offering visitors free admission to their permanent collection. Once attracted, visitors are likely to return regularly if the museum interprets its materials skillfully.

In order to fulfill the museum's educational mission, those who plan interpretive exhibits, lectures, and workshops should themselves have some training in the humanities. We suggest that universities and museums develop collaborative programs for training museum personnel and familiarizing academic humanists with the methods of museum work. Misunderstandings between faculty in the humanities and museum personnel have traditionally blocked collaboration between universities and art museums. This barrier seems to be dissolving as graduates in the humanities seek careers in museums, and college faculty and museum personnel realize that they have something to offer each other. Museums want to be able to call upon humanists who can help relate collections to broad cultural themes. The NEH, State Humanities Committees, American Association of Museums (AAM), Association of Science-Technology Centers, and American Association for State and Local History can provide an important and inexpensive service by furthering consultation between college faculty and museum staffs—by such means as the AAM's recent series of seminars, Lifelong Learning in the Humanities, in which museum professionals, adult educators, and university humanists discussed methods of interpretation and other ways of using museum resources in adult programs in the humanities.

RECOMMENDATION 20: Federal support for general operating expenses of museums should expand through increased appropriations not only for the Institute of Museum Services and the Challenge Grant Programs of both Endowments, but also for project grants from the NEH, NEA, and National Science Foundation; private sources of support should provide more funds for general operating expenses.

Their growing popularity and the inflationary costs of conservation and maintenance cause serious problems for museums. Educational projects, many of them developed over the last decade with support from the two National Endowments and private sources, have become a regular and expensive part of museums' operations. In general, the public demand for services exceeds the financial resources of museums. Museums cite conservation, storage, security, and building maintenance as their most pressing concerns. On the basis of a recent Museum Universe Survey conducted by the federal Institute of Museum Services (IMS) and the National Center for Education Statistics, the IMS estimates that the total annual operating budget of American museums approaches the $1 billion mark—this notwithstanding the fact that over half of all museum personnel are unpaid volunteers (information provided by the IMS).

Federal funds for museums are administered by a number of agencies: the two Endowments; the National Science Foundation; the National Museum Act (Smithsonian Institution); and the Institute of Museum Services (Department of Education). The responsibility for federal support of museums should be shared among these agencies, whose policies should consider interpretive programs as necessary operations. The Endowments' Challenge Grants and the Institute's grants for general operations provide the most broadly based support for operating expenses. Chances are fair to good that the funds available from these sources will increase over the next few years, continuing the past decade's upward trend in federal support of museums. But coordination among federal agencies is a problem, as we shall point out in the next chapter, and the needs of museums outstrip what federal sources can provide. The NEH has awarded Challenge Grants to about 65 percent of the applicants from museums of various kinds. But many museums (especially smaller ones with small staffs) cannot find sufficient outside funds to meet the three-to-one ratio required for a Challenge Grant, and no museum is allowed more than one such grant; we think that the ratio should be reduced where appropriate, and that the restriction to one grant should be relaxed. The seventeen hundred proposals submitted to the IMS for fiscal year (FY) 1979 requested a total of $27.5 million, but the agency had only $7.8 million to dispense, and some institutions (e.g., small historical societies) do not meet the IMS's definition of a museum even when their functions include cataloging and conservation.

While arguing for increased Congressional appropriations for museums, we hope that federal support will stimulate greater support for museums from their local communities through memberships, volunteers, school programs, state and municipal funds, and private philanthropy. The responsibility for public education in the humanities is a collective one.

Public Libraries

The public library is the single most important cultural institution in most communities, and preserving its vitality is unequivocally in the national interest. Inside their walls and through outreach programs, public libraries have traditionally provided services to a wide range of users—reference and research, circulation of materials, reading programs for children, lectures and discussion groups for adults, and so on. Like museums, many libraries have added new services in recent years to meet growing public needs. Libraries, teachers of the humanities, and the many readers of library books are learning from each other how books and other library resources can enrich private and community life.

RECOMMENDATION 21: To encourage greater public use of their resources in the humanities, libraries should expand their educational programs, seek the participation of humanists in the planning of these programs, and improve the independent learner's access to collections.

To serve adult learners, many public libraries have developed extensive counseling programs and act as educational referral agencies. Some offer groups of readers an opportunity to study a common theme. Libraries also assist adults in designing independent study programs and direct them to credit or degree-granting programs. Many libraries offer resources for computer-aided instruction and facilities for the use of videocassettes and videodiscs. Especially in art, theater, and other subjects where visual experience is essential, video technologies can provide library users of all ages with entertaining and informative access to the humanities. According to a recent study of cooperative programs between community colleges and public libraries, a few libraries have organized learning laboratories with the support of local community colleges to bring new technologies for self-instruction to the adult learner (American Association of Community and Junior Colleges and the Public Library Association, *Research Report: Community Colleges, Public Libraries, and the Humanities,* Washington, D.C., 1978).

• One approach to adult educational services with an explicit focus on the humanities is that of the Houston Public Library, which tailors its programs to particular community concerns. The library encourages adults to read about and discuss common interests and sponsors lectures, displays, and study guides on local topics such as city architecture. Its programs on general themes, such as Death, Dying, and Grief, draw on the perspectives of ethnic groups in the community. Faculty from local colleges and universities join librarians in preparing annotated reading lists for adults wishing to pursue a topic.

• For help in setting up outreach programs for adults who are illiterate or who speak English as a second language, a number of libraries have turned to the Literacy Volunteers of America (LVA) in Syracuse, New York, which has affiliated programs in twenty-one states. With LVA's assistance, libraries provide training for volunteers as well as materials and facilities for teaching.

• Libraries in several cities offer the College Without Walls program, which helps independent learners define their educational goals using the library as the main resource. This program also advises eligible participants about the College Board's College Level Examination Program, which enables students to receive college credit for nonformal education.

Unfortunately, library programs are often taken for granted. Though few people openly oppose libraries, equally few actively support them—at least not until their own library is threatened. In many communities, budgetary constraints have forced public libraries to restrict their services and limit their hours of operation.

RECOMMENDATION 22: Communities must keep public libraries open and preserve access to library services. Local and state governments must support public libraries by every means available. We recommend that federal support for public libraries increase in a way that neither discourages local and state support nor intrudes on the operations of local libraries.

Library revenues fall far short of the cost of operations, according to studies of the National Commission on Libraries and Information Science. Because public libraries depend heavily on local funding (about 80 percent of total funds in 1975), they are especially vulnerable to the financial repercussions of tax cuts. Of course libraries must be accountable to the taxpayer. But too often their services are viewed as nonessential and are cut before (or more drastically than) other public services. This attitude represents an appalling social and political bankruptcy. No community or state can afford to curb its citizens' access to ideas and information. Nor should local or state officials look to the federal government to finance the bulk of this essential public service.

A major shift away from local funding might weaken the public library's intimate relationship with the community and discourage local initiatives. Funds from private foundations have enabled the New York Public Library to stay open one or two evenings a week. In California many individuals and some local businesses have supported libraries explicitly to help offset recent budget cuts. Some communities have rallied aid for their libraries; in Toledo and Tulsa, for example, tax referendums passed following massive campaigns for public support. Although such support may be viewed as an emergency measure, it is also an encouraging sign. Some communities value their libraries highly. That value can be made still more visible—as many State Humanities Committees recognize—through collaboration between libraries and other cultural and educational institutions. Collaboration between public libraries, community college libraries, and school libraries should be particularly encouraged, to avoid wasteful duplication of resources and improve services. Coordination might be especially economical for acquisition of expensive materials and computerized methods of cataloging and searching.

Federal support for public libraries includes funds authorized by the Library Services and Construction Act (LSCA), administered by the Department of Education, and grants made by the NEH. LSCA grants are awarded to states to improve access to library services and encourage networking among libraries. The Endowment's Public Library Program, established in the Division of Public Programs in 1978, supports the development of programs in the humanities and encourages public use of library resources. The most critical need of many libraries, however, as of many museums, is for funds to cover general operating costs. While NEH Challenge Grants may be used for this purpose, the Endowment made only twelve such awards to public libraries from 1976 to May 1979—in part because it received few applications. The National Library Act pending in Congress and the White House Conference on Library and Information Services of November 1979 indicate growing federal concern for public libraries. An increase in federal support may be politically feasible, especially if the government recognizes preservation as a major operating expense for libraries and a major federal responsibility. While an increased federal role will not solve local funding problems, it might enable libraries to economize in some areas—such as bibliographic systems and networking—and direct more funds to local programs.

Historical Organizations

Historical organizations vary considerably in type, size, and function, ranging from state-supported historical societies with budgets in the millions of dollars to tiny local committees with no paid staff or permanent facilities. Whatever their differences, all historical organizations express by their very nature the spirit of respect for the past that infuses humanistic activity. According to the director of the American Association for State and Local History (AASLH), testifying on the proposed White House Conference on the Humanities, local historical societies may be the closest thing to a national network of humanistic organizations (*Joint Hearings*, 9 January 1978). That network has grown in recent decades; in 1950, for example, there were 59 historical societies in the state of Wisconsin, today some 170.

Historical organizations have traditionally served America by preserving the materials of our heritage and disseminating knowledge about our past. In the wake of the Bicentennial and television's "Roots," there has been a resurgence of interest in American history and personal origins. Russell Fridley, Director of the Minnesota Historical Society, wrote us that public interest in history "has never been higher, and the public is turning to historical societies to offer courses outside the traditional academic environment." This interest is still one more index of Americans' active participation in the humanities. Whether tracing a family genealogy, reading a biography of Henry VIII, or participating in an archeological dig, personal engagement with history marks a fruitful path toward self-knowledge.

RECOMMENDATION 23: To improve public use and understanding of the records of our past, historical organizations and the agencies that support them—notably the Department of the Interior and the NEH, but also state governments and private agencies—should concentrate on developing programs connecting preservation with interpretation.

Ideally, historical preservation should have a living use. Historical organizations have an obligation to serve the personal interests of individuals and help communities reach a shared self-awareness. Those public organizations identified as the official representatives of a city, state, or region should elucidate the contributions made by all racial and ethnic groups to the history of the area. Buildings and sites worthy of preservation are also worthy of interpretation. Documents and historical materials can stimulate informal learning as well as professional research and academic curricula. Many institutions and communities, with the cooperation of local museums and historical organizations, have started to put local historical resources to use.

• At Middle Tennessee State University, the Mid-South Humanities Project seeks to revitalize student interest in literature and history with curricula drawing on local and regional historical resources. High school and community college teachers from eight states form demonstration teams to design courses for their regions. They attend a training institute where speakers from the Smithsonian, the National Trust for Historic Preservation, and the American Association for State and Local History join specialists in folklore, architecture, and other fields in discussing how to use local resources for teaching the humanities. In one course, for example, students studied the effects of the Great Depression on local culture through folk songs, photographs, and oral history interviews.

• In the Bedford-Stuyvesant area of Brooklyn, members of the community participated in the collection and restoration of artifacts from the mid-1800s, when Bedford-Stuyvesant was a free Black community called Weeksville. While learning about their cultural past, residents of all ages, including schoolchildren, developed pride in their local heritage and new interests in history. The Society for the Preservation of Weeksville has acquired old houses for a museum and educational center to carry on historical work in the community.

Sources of support for historical organizations are various—membership and visitors' fees, gift shop revenues, private philanthropy, municipal funds, annual state budget appropriations, and federal agencies. Several programs of the NEH emphasize the interpretation of state and local history. One of three main grant categories in the General Research Program of the Division of Research Grants is that of State, Local, and Regional History Projects. With a budget of $1.5 million for FY1980, this program encourages participation by members of historical societies and museums. As a Bicentennial project, the Division of Research Grants subsidized the preparation of state histories under the administration of the AASLH. The Endowment's Division of Public Programs also supports the activities of historical organizations through its Museums and Historical Organizations Program, which has a budget of $8.5 million for FY1980. Although many of the State Humanities Committees are developing an interest in local history, in 1978 only one-fourth of all state grants for such projects went to historical societies.

Further federal support comes from a division of the National

Archives, the National Historic Publications and Records Commission (NHPRC). With a budget of $4 million in FY1980 allocated through each state's archives, the NHPRC "encourages a greater effort at all levels of government and by private organizations to preserve and make available for use those records, generated in every facet of life, that further an understanding and appreciation of American history" (NHPRC, *Records Program Guidelines and Procedures: Applications and Grants*, Washington, D.C., 1979). The NHPRC and the Collections Program of the Endowment's Research Division complement each other, and there is coordination between them.

In 1949 Congress chartered the National Trust for Historic Preservation, a unique private organization, "to lead the movement for preservation of our architectural and historic resources." It places special emphasis on "preservation education." Commendably, its Education Services Division broadly interprets preservation as including activities in the arts and humanities that focus on local architecture and historic sites. The National Trust grants funds for educational projects in schools and colleges and publishes guides to help historical organizations improve their educational programs.

The National Trust receives funding on a matching basis from the Heritage Conservation and Recreation Service (HCRS) in the Department of the Interior. But most federal support defines preservation in a narrow sense so as to neglect interpretation. The Historic Preservation Fund ($55 million appropriated for FY1980), administered by HCRS and apportioned among the states through the State Historic Preservation Officers, is spent on the acquisition and restoration of historic and cultural properties. (What is acquired or restored must be listed with the National Register.) Following this lead, many historical organizations sponsor the restoration and preservation of historic sites and buildings rather than their interpretation or use by scholars or the public.

Historical organizations sorely need help to train personnel, especially since many of them rely on volunteer staff. According to the AASLH, one-fifth of its over four thousand member organizations have no paid staff. Federal support for training is inadequate. The NEH ended its program for museum staff development in 1978, and no new program has emerged to fill this need. The National Museum Act supports some professional training and related activities, such as the AASLH's consultant services. But funding for the Act, $714,000 in FY1980, falls far short of the needs of the field, and it stresses preservation, not interpretive skills.

Humanists in residence with historical organizations can help compensate for the lack of professional staff. In New York, for example, the Cornell Historical Resources Center, with a grant from the New York Council for the Humanities and the New York Council on the Arts, has placed historians with historical societies to help develop interpretive programs. Humanists should themselves learn about the techniques of preservation. The AASLH, NEH, and State Humanities Committees should cooperate in identifying humanists with appropriate interests and talents for work with historical organizations.

Historic preservation is indispensable for understanding the past. Historical organizations need and deserve support for placing our material heritage into the cultural and historical context that gives it meaning. Both public and private agencies should increase their support for the interpretation of historical resources, which should be available to all interested citizens for educational and recreational purposes.

MEDIA

Although television, radio, and newspapers are not institutions of the same order as the others we have considered in this chapter, their educational functions are similar. Like colleges, they offer instruction in many fields. They provide a record, not wholly unlike that kept by museums and libraries, of history—most often, of course, as it unfolds. In ways occasionally humanistic in form, often humanistic in spirit, the media describe and interpret the world. People learn from the media—or, on occasion, are denied the opportunity to learn when that would be entirely possible.

Television and Radio

The electronic media, especially television, have changed how many people learn. With considerable sophistication, television controls our perception of its message, shaping what we learn from it as it determines our manner of learning. Television is a potent rival of traditional methods of acquiring information from books, discussions, and lectures, especially among young people who, it has been estimated, spend at least as many hours watching television as attending school. No less than the form, the content of television programming has affected traditional concerns of the humanities—language, perceptions of politics and citizenship, and social values and individual behavior. For entertainment and information, television and its sister art, film, have taken their places beside reading in our culture. Through dramatic and documentary forms, these arts can convey to millions of people at once a uniform impression of how men and women behave. For many people broadcasts have become the principal source of information regarding current events.

The profound social and cultural power of the electronic media requires that we develop a critical sense of how they are used. As suggested elsewhere in this report, our educational institutions must take into account the new learning styles created by the electronic media—habits of mind that have become as natural to many people as the textual and historical modes of thought characteristic of traditional, literate culture. Intelligently used, the media can enrich education and increase participation in the humanities. The humanities in turn are essential for developing a critical eye for judging what the media offer.

Many recent programs of the Public Broadcasting Service (PBS), such as "Dance in America," "The American Short Story," and "The Ascent of Man," have shown that television can serve the humanities and arts effectively. The growth of public television—in funding (a fourfold increase in the budget of the Corporation for Public Broadcasting, CPB, since 1970) and in the size of its audience—indicates that there is considerable interest in a satisfying alternative to commercial television. The commercial networks themselves have produced popular programs on historical and ethical themes ("Roots" and "Holocaust," for example). As an entertainment medium serving its sponsors, however, commercial television is not likely to offer extensive programming in the arts and humanities. This goal, we believe, can best be reached through greater diversity in the programs shown on television.

With the advent of new technologies in telecommunications, an enormous diversification of television programming is in fact on the horizon. Multi-channel cable service, satellite distribution systems, and videocassette and videodisc equipment have already started to transform the entire communications industry. About one-fifth of American households subscribe to cable systems carrying up to thirty-six channels, and one million new subscribers join annually. Nearly one-quarter of the cable systems now in place receive all or part of their programming by satellite transmission. Rapidly growing channel space and the relatively low cost of satellite distribution promise a favorable economic environment for the development of new programming services. Video recorders and players give viewers more control over their television sets. Prerecorded videodisc products may become a multi-billion-dollar industry in the next decade.

Increased options for the viewer do not guarantee programs of high quality in the arts and humanities. Defenders and critics of commercial television have observed that the sheer quantity of programming needed to fill the broadcast day tends to reduce the quality of what is produced. As more producers enter the field, competition for dollars to develop programming will probably increase; at the same time, competition for programming and the talent that creates it will drive up costs of production. Cable services, in which the viewer pays on a per-program or per-channel basis for special programming, could sustain an all-opera or all-drama network, and some performing arts organizations such as the Lincoln Center are investigating the possibilities of producing works for this kind of distribution. Such efforts will not necessarily bring diverse cultural programming to as many homes as want it.

For the presentation of humanistic subjects and themes, radio is less expensive than TV and its scheduling more flexible. Radio may also more easily accommodate learning in the humanities—by focusing intensely on ideas or challenging the listener's imagination. In the presentation of news, for example, it can include commentary and analysis that do not have to compete with images for the listener's attention. Radio is more compatible with the use of a printed text than is television, as anyone knows who has followed a score while listening to opera.

• National Public Radio (NPR, the association of public radio stations funded by the Corporation for Public Broadcasting) has produced "A Question of Place," a series of portraits of important figures in cultural history such as James Joyce and Claude Lévi-Strauss. This project was supported by the National Endowment for the Humanities, as was NPR's series on F. Scott Fitzgerald. With support from the Wisconsin Humanities Committee, radio station WHA of the University of Wisconsin-Extension in Madison has developed programming in the humanities including daily commentaries, occasional interviews, and monthly call-in forums on current issues and historical and literary themes; all feature faculty in the humanities from universities around the state.

The public broadcasting establishment will continue to bear a major responsibility for producing cultural programs on radio and television. The changing technological environment of American telecommunications will surely have a significant—though now somewhat unpredictable—impact on public and commercial broadcasting. Congress plans to rewrite the now badly outmoded Federal Communications Act; new regulations will affect the quality of broadcast programming in future decades. The recent Carnegie Commission on the Future of Public Broadcasting ("Carnegie II") has made recommendations on the administrative and financial needs of public broadcasting, but what influence their findings will have on Congress or public broadcasting officials is not yet clear.

We urge that in any design for improving public broadcasting services adequate resources be reserved for the humanities and arts. In the meantime, those involved in noncommercial broadcasting—including government officials, sources of support, and independent producers and stations—should give attention to the major problems that currently plague cultural programming: insufficient funds, the bureaucratic tangles often faced by producers seeking funds, and the need to insure local control over programming decisions.

Programs for the media are expensive; major television productions for national broadcast can cost millions of dollars, and while both National Endowments have helped sponsor good and relatively popular programs, their resources are limited. The annual budget of the NEH's Media Programs (Division of Public Programs) has grown dramatically from $0.2 million in its first year to $9.1 million in 1980; but the Endowment staff notes that $100 million would be needed to complete just a fraction of the better projects submitted.

Because of their high cost and visibility, major television programs are relatively risky ventures for public agencies held accountable for spending taxpayers' money wisely. To minimize such risks, the NEH relies on step-funding procedures in underwriting productions; to insure that programs have an authentic humanistic quality, the NEH ordinarily requires that academic specialists in the humanities participate in production decisions. To producers and media artists, however, these procedures can present bureaucratic, artistic, and financial problems that make production difficult at best. The underwriting of public broadcasting, whether by corporations, foundations, or government agencies, raises questions of censorship and control of the public airwaves. Carnegie II observes, "Corporate underwriting has undoubtedly skewed the total schedule in the direction of cultural programs which are popular among the 'upscale' audience that corporations prefer. Controversial drama, documentaries, public affairs, and programs for minority and other special audiences must then compete for remaining discretionary money" (*A Public Trust*, New York, 1979). But some observers contend that the same skewing also results from government grants, and that corporate underwriting has in fact recently been obtained for a few programs in public affairs, such as the "MacNeil-Lehrer Report."

A related issue is that of local versus national control of programming. In the PBS network, for example, nearly three hundred member stations vote on what shows they want. Critics contend that this procedure makes it difficult for new shows, or shows of only local or regional interest, to reach the air. Recently, PBS expanded its programming into three separate services transmitted by satellite. One carries high visibility programs with broad appeal; another offers special interest and regional programs as well as works of independent producers; and the third provides educational services. Through the three-part system, stations will have a wider variety of programs to choose from when trying to meet local needs. In the same spirit, the NEH's Media Programs section and many State Humanities Committees make grants to individual radio and television stations for the development of programs appropriate for local or regional audiences.

Carnegie II has proposed a sizable increase in the financing of public broadcasting, to nearly $1.2 billion by 1985, and a more even balance among funding sources—the federal government, state and local sources, foundations and corporations, and the individual stations themselves—in order to insulate producers and programmers from undue influence by the government or any other agent. Moreover, Carnegie II suggests that federal funds be granted directly to individual stations rather than through the system's central bodies (CPB, PBS, NPR) as at present. According to the Carnegie Commission, most funds for public broadcasting should be raised and spent locally to protect the autonomy of stations in the production and selection of programs. This autonomy is also the goal of the Commission's major recommendations regarding the structural reorganization of the public broadcasting system, notably its proposed Program Services Endowment.

More money and autonomy for a reorganized public broadcasting system may help create more media programs in the arts and humanities. Such changes will not necessarily guarantee the quality of programs, nor promote the many uses beyond broadcasting that we believe good programs can serve.

RECOMMENDATION 24:   Insuring the best use of available resources and outlets for radio, television, and film presentations of the humanities will require the collaboration of public and private sources of support, educational and cultural institutions, media experts, and humanists. Sources of support should permit more experimentation in the development of media programs. Educational and cultural institutions can explore connections with public broadcasting stations and commercial systems, such as cable, in order to enhance their services to the public. Ongoing cooperation is needed between media experts and humanists in the study of uses of the electronic media.

Public and philanthropic support of media programs should help set standards of quality and diversity for the commercial media and the public. Large, high-risk ventures—media "blockbusters"—are one means to this end, but not the only one. Indeed, some would argue that the stepfunding used to reduce the risks in such productions leads to programming by committee, adding to costs without necessarily improving the product. In fact, as some producers in the media contend, too narrow a focus on programs puts unnecessary limits on the uses of the media for the humanities. The electronic media cover the humanities by their very nature, and not necessarily only through specific programs. More general or discretionary support for the humanities in broadcasting could help radio and television exploit everyday opportunities for dealing with humanistic themes—for instance, by providing historical or analytical commentaries on current events or on recently broadcast programs. Diversity achieved through more experimentation and through more, and perhaps smaller, risks is the most promising avenue for the humanities in the electronic media.

For the humanities, the potentials of the media are not limited to broadcasting—another reason for broader diversity and experimentation. Tapes and films should be considered permanent and easily preserved resources, with many uses in formal and nonformal education. Many schools, colleges, and universities are increasing their use of electronic media facilities. Several public broadcasting stations are based on college campuses. Individual institutions and consortia offer courses to local and distant learners through cable and public television. Video recording and playback devices allow creative uses of media materials in the classroom; in tutored video instruction (TVI), for example, a teacher can act as mediator between students and a recorded lecture, drama, or other material, stopping the action on the screen for questions and discussion as necessary.

Video recordings promise to change our conception of a library, whether in the community, college, school, or home. With the coupling of computer and telecommunications technologies, the everyday uses of electronic recordings of information will multiply. So will the opportunities for learning and enjoyment in the humanities—but only if humanists and media experts work together in exploring how the media and the humanities can serve each other. There is little such collaboration at present. Media artists need to know more about the subjects and methods of humanistic disciplines; conversely, humanists need to understand how materials for the media are put together. Whether television and radio programs on the humanities are developed for commercial or public broadcast, or for use in the home or classroom, humanists should participate in their production from the beginning.

• An NEH planning grant to KPBS in San Diego may be a promising model for increasing understanding between humanists and the media while expanding the humanistic content of local programming. The grant covered the cost of opening and staffing a Humanities Office at the station. According to the station's report of what the grant accomplished, "the experiment clearly demonstrated the feasibility of training an academic humanist to become a television producer, but it also showed that the process can have an immediate strengthening impact for local and regional humanities television programming" (information provided by KPBS).

There has been considerable discussion recently of the need for a center to study the place of the media in our culture. The University of Southern California Center for the Humanities, the Aspen Institute for Humanistic Studies, and several other organizations are particularly interested in connections between the humanities and media. The Federation of Public Programs in the

Humanities (an association of State Humanities Committees) is conducting a study of the uses of the media in programs of public education in the humanities and compiling a catalog of available media materials. Such activities may provide a base for continued discussion and expanded use of radio and television programs on the humanities.

Newspapers

Like radio, newspapers are implicitly humanistic. Through analysis and commentary on the news of the day, they provide cultural and historical background for a broad public readership. Articles on local history, foreign countries, and breakthroughs in science and technology; reviews of books and the arts; reports on important cultural events: these forms of journalism deal with themes from the humanities.

Traditionally, newspapers' first consideration has been the news, and the humanities are often old news indeed. As a result of competition from the instantaneous news services of the broadcast media, however, many newspapers give more space than they did before to background and analysis of the news, social and cultural commentary, and feature stories—opportunities for expanding coverage of the humanities in print. Readers seem eager for newspapers to explore their educational potential, and some editors claim that they would welcome more well-written articles and essays by humanists.

• Courses by Newspaper (CbN), developed by the University of California Extension at San Diego and supported by the NEH and the California Council for the Humanities, has demonstrated that there is an audience for newspaper articles on humanistic themes. Each year since 1973, CbN has offered two series of weekly essays by scholars in the humanities on various issues of public concern. CbN materials are carried by over 450 newspapers nationwide, and have been used as the basis for academic courses in some 300 colleges and universities. Most recently, CbN has become an integral part of "national issues forums" in which community colleges cooperate with local libraries, museums, and other institutions to promote public discussion of the humanistic dimensions of timely public concerns.

Newspapers have been a medium of education and entertainment far longer than radio and television, but the value of newspapers is overshadowed by the debate over the social force of the electronic media. At the heart of this debate is a question that is profoundly humanistic: what effects do radio and television have on education and culture? The impact of the media on our society can only grow as their uses diversify. As schools and higher education look ahead to scarce financial resources and increasingly complex demands for educational services, will "teleducation" include learning in the humanities? Will the home videodisc libraries of the 1990s include humanistic materials? Affirmative answers are in the national interest, and they depend on the willingness of scholars and teachers in the humanities to use the electronic media as well as the printed page.

Americans are becoming increasingly aware of material limits in both public and private life. These limits will affect our cultural life, which, like the windmill, must turn in order to generate. Our culture is sustained by the institutions and activities described in this chapter. The steady impetus they provide should not be shut off by internal policies or external limits imposed upon them.

CHAPTER FIVE 🌿

Support for the Humanities

If I'd as much money as I could spend,
I never would cry old chairs to mend. . . .
(Nursery Rhyme)

The humanities cannot realistically expect large increases in funding in the 1980s, during a period of widespread retrenchment. Yet institutions and individuals serving the humanities are vulnerable to rising costs and to the demand for accountability. Inflation and taxes have underlined the need for fiscal accountability across the board; but tax-cutting measures slash budgets arbitrarily and can too easily result in diminished support for the humanities. In the preceding chapters we have argued that the humanities are essential to our national life. In a time of shortage they and their benefactors must uphold what is of greatest value.

Applicants for support will have to continue living with sharp contrasts between levels of federal funding for the humanities and the sciences—the combined budgets of the Humanities and Arts Endowments in 1980 amount to less than a third of that of the National Science Foundation. Scientists can justify support of research because it might some day yield industrial benefits. Many humanistic institutions, such as the American Council of Learned Societies (ACLS), museums, and independent research libraries, are searching energetically for several sources of support. This search is necessary. But what effects will it have on the mission and staff resources of any given institution? How will the need for support affect what individual applicants write or teach? These questions about the interdependency of culture and funding are not new, but they become particularly urgent whenever the number of applicants for available funds becomes disproportionately large. Such is the case today and will be probably for at least the next decade. In this situation, sources of support have a special obligation to assess their impact on the humanities.

Both applicants and sources must weigh short-term against long-term needs. There is an immediate and continuing need to connect the humanities to the everyday concerns of more people. We must also look beyond the 1980s. The vitality of the humanities and American culture in the next century will depend on how well we educate our children today, how adequately we support scholarship and teaching, and how intelligently we preserve our educational and cultural institutions.

The growth of the National Endowment for the Humanities (NEH) attests to the acceptance of a federal responsibility for helping sustain the cultural life of our nation. But no one can overemphasize the importance of maintaining a variety of sources of support. As John W. Gardner points out, "The private pursuit of public purpose is an honored tradition in American life. We do not regard the furtherance of public purpose as a monopoly of government. And that belief has released incredible human energy and commitment in behalf of the community" (*Chronicle of Higher Education*, 8 January 1979).

The apparent advantages of private philanthropy over federal or state funding are many. Private giving provides multiple centers of initiative and response, and often attaches fewer political and bureaucratic strings to grants. It can allow more freedom for innovative and controversial projects and can be more sensitive to the special needs of communities.

American private philanthropy in 1978 totaled an estimated $39.56 billion in current dollars, compared to $16.81 billion in 1968. In real purchasing power, however, the gain was only about 18 percent; in 1978 the dollar bought a little more than half of what it had ten years earlier. In 1978 individuals contributed $32.8 billion (or 82.9 percent of the total); bequests $2.6 billion (6.5 percent); foundations $2.16 billion (5.5 percent); corporations $2 billion (5.1 percent). Approximately $5.52 billion went to education (including about $3.04 billion to higher education), and $2.49 billion to the arts and humanities as activities separate from education. Individual contributions accounted for roughly half of private support for higher education and well over half of such support for the arts and humanities (American Association of Fund-Raising Counsel, Inc., *Giving USA: 1979 Annual Report,* New York).

These statistics show the magnitude of "the private pursuit of public purpose" in this country. They imply how grievously this pursuit would suffer if individual giving declined, whether because of government tax policy or a loss of faith in philanthropy; the increase in the standard tax deduction discourages charitable contributions, and the future of private philanthropy could be seriously affected by "sunset" bills reviewing tax laws currently favorable to charitable deductions. Although most of the recommendations in this report are directed to institutions or organizations, we hope we have also given individuals good cause to maintain their remarkable contribution to the commonweal.

In previous chapters we have made specific recommendations for support, offering at least implicit guidance to people who spend and give monies. The recommendations in this chapter may also assist applicants, but are intended chiefly for sources of support—particularly foundations, corporations, and federal agencies.

PROBLEMS OF SUPPORT

No single rule applies with equal validity to all foundations, corporations, and federal agencies. No systematic data clearly indicate levels, patterns, and sources of funding for educational and cultural institutions. Mechanisms should be established to collect and analyze such data. The NEH has begun to do this, and should consider establishing a network among major educational, scholarly, and cultural associations, tying into the chief data bases for federal and private giving. Meanwhile, the lack of complete evidence need not prevent our tentatively identifying five problems that apply to specific sources of support and that the recommendations at the end of this section may help solve.

In the first place, the humanities are difficult to define and classify. Most foundations and corporations, if they do identify the humanities, support them chiefly as arts and culture—with emphasis on the performing arts and museums. Certainly the humanities encompass the arts, but the results of artistic activity are easier to see than the effects of an interpretive exhibit, book, public forum, or academic course. Thus, neither the aggregate of support for art and culture nor climbing attendance figures for the performing arts can be interpreted as widespread support for the humanities in general, or as recognition of their importance in our culture. On the other hand, many public and private sources without an explicit category of funding for the humanities do support them—through grants for general education and professional curricula, faculty development, research libraries, the media, and so on.

Second, internal policies and procedures complicate funding. Sources of funds distinguish between programs, discretionary grants, general operating expenses, endowment, capital improvement, preservation, and so forth. To the applicant, such distinctions sometimes appear rigid, for these functions are interwoven in many institutions. A related problem is that of overhead expenses—the percentage allowed varies widely depending on the nature of the programs and the source of funds (the government generally accepting higher overhead than do private donors). Many private and federal sources hesitate to pay operating expenses or to fund programs of more than three years. Brochures and lists of grants normally show preference for seeding new projects rather than sustaining old ones, even when the latter have proven their effectiveness.

These internal policies are neither misanthropic nor wholly unwarranted. Sources of support have their own sense of social and cultural mission. They want applicants to specify how they will use the money. The staffs are themselves accountable to governing boards, stockholders, or the electorate, and often overloaded with applications. Still, internal policies and preferences can overemphasize innovation and increase the intricacies and hypocrisy of grantsmanship, causing applicants to disguise real but routine needs as exciting new departures. Policies burden even successful applicants with the time-consuming paperwork of frequent proposals. Carried to extremes, the policies of the grantor can deny the recipient of the grant sufficient latitude to spend money wisely.

Third, the complex relationship between private and federal sources is relatively unexplored. The connection has become all the more important with the increasing use of matching and Challenge Grants by the National Endowment for the Humanities. Some private donors have assumed that the NEH can carry most of the load. Recently the Rockefeller Foundation pointed out that the increasing pressure on the NEH to emphasize public programs could make more important the contributions of private foundations to other areas such as scholarship (*1977 Annual Report,* New York). We note with regret the virtual loss of two long-time supporters of advanced study in the humanities. Although the Ford Foundation supports research libraries and liberal arts colleges, it has curtailed its funding of the humanities since 1971 and its support for the ACLS postdoctoral fellowship program expires in 1981–82. The Danforth Foundation will end its graduate fellowships by the mid-1980s.

We are also concerned about gaps or imbalances in funding particular areas of the humanities. Private and government funding sources often pass in the dark or resort to reasoning whereby each expects the other to sustain successful programs, when in fact both stress innovation and frequently decline requests for essential operating expenses. More recently we have observed—and strongly recommend—an increasing degree of cooperation between private and federal sources. Both recognize the need to help applicants develop their own long-term funding strategies, and both know that imbalances will be hard to rectify for some years to come.

Fourth, foundations, corporations, and the NEH expect the humanities to go before the public both financially and intellectually, often by means of new projects. We agree that the humanities will have to seek funds from a larger variety of sources than is now the case, and that they can often relate research, teaching, and collections of materials to contemporary public concerns. But the humanities should not always be pressed to connect interpretations of the past with issues of the present. Interpretation of humanistic materials and public outreach are signal responsibilities for the humanities. They are also opportunities for humanists and cultural institutions to show the vitality of scholarship, teaching, and artifacts even when they are not directly related to contemporary issues or values. Often these opportunities should be seized through innovative projects. In our society, however, innovation often connotes a "new, improved" product or a quick adaptation to changing public moods. Sources of support for the humanities should not reinforce these connotations. Doing so can damage the humanities' roots in the past, disregard the often slow process by which research filters into public consciousness, strain the custodial mission of institutions, and narrow the public conception of our national culture.

A final problem is evaluation. Most sources of support periodically review their policies and have procedures for evaluating projects they have funded. Rarely do they assess their own impact on what they call "the field"—the teachers, scholars, students, institutions, and others who apply for funds. No federal agency or private organization monitors broad trends or policies of support. No one looks critically and comprehensively at gaps in the support system or at the effects that varying levels of funding have on the educational and cultural needs described in this report.

RECOMMENDATION 25: All sources of funds, from state legislatures to private philanthropy, should give effect to the fundamental importance of the humanities in nurturing the quality of American education and community life. No educational philosophy or cultural policy is whole without the humanities, and therefore the humanities must be a line item in institutional budgets, philanthropy, and public consciousness. Sources should not expect applicants to translate requests for support into marketing terminology, for the value of the humanities cannot be measured by quantifiable standards of productivity.

RECOMMENDATION 26: Sources should assess their programs to determine how much they actually support the humanities and how they might better do so. These assessments can seek to achieve the following: more precise classifications of grant categories; recognition of areas of funding where some aspect of the humanities relates to their programs even though without an explicitly humanistic label (e.g., liberal education, the arts, ethics, communications, critical thinking); identification of the peculiar characteristics and needs of the humanities; guidelines for increasing support to the humanities in a manner compatible with the source's mission or an expanded perception of that mission. Sources should keep these assessments on file for the information of applicants and for use in surveys of patterns of support.

RECOMMENDATION 27:   Sources should review their policies and procedures with these objectives in view: an increase in broadly defined or unrestricted grants, and a loosening of distinctions between kinds of grants (programs, operating expenses, etc.); more frequent grants to sustain successful programs and reduce requirements for time-consuming annual proposals; if sustaining grants or funds for operating expenses are unfeasible, then at least some support for overhead costs.

RECOMMENDATION 28:   Public and private sources need to establish adequate collaboration in order to identify priorities for funding by major types of sources; avoid so much overlap in some areas of funding (e.g., public programs for adults) that other areas suffer (e.g., elementary and secondary education); assess the effects of general trends or policies of support on broad fields of applicants; discuss means for increasing the number of unrestricted or sustaining grants; foster the pooling of small grants; assess the availability of private funds for matching federal grants. The current mode of collaboration—chiefly *ad hoc* consultation—is insufficient. We recommend that representatives from foundations and corporations with major commitments to the humanities, and from such organizations as the Council for Financial Aid to Education, American Association for the Advancement of the Humanities, and NEH meet periodically to discuss these and related issues. This joint committee on support should not become so large as to inhibit discussions of long-range planning, but it should solicit advice from a wide range of educational and cultural constituencies.

SOURCES OF SUPPORT

Each of the three major sources of support in this chapter has peculiar characteristics. We discuss foundations first because they have the longest tradition of funding the humanities. Corporations have a much larger capacity to increase their contributions than do foundations. The National Endowment for the Humanities symbolizes public acceptance of the principle that supporting the humanities is in the national interest. All three can improve their record of support; in the recommendations at the end of the chapter we suggest how they may do so in a manner compatible with their respective missions.

Foundations

Uncertain data and varied models confound any assessment of foundation support for the humanities. In current dollars, foundation giving increased from $1.6 billion in 1968 to $2.16 billion in 1978. In constant (1968) dollars, however, the 1978 total was worth only $1.14 billion, representing an actual decline in purchasing power of nearly half a billion during the ten years—striking evidence of erosion caused by inflation (*The Foundation Directory*, 6th and 7th eds., New York, 1978 and 1979).

Of the seven major areas of funding identified by the Foundation Center (education, health, sciences, welfare, humanities, international activities, and religion), education was the largest in the period 1975–78 and the humanities in fifth or sixth place. In 1978 alone, foundations reporting by field of interest contributed $233 million to education, or 28 percent of their grants. As a rough estimate (for many education grants are not classified by field), disciplines in the humanities and arts received between 15 and 20 percent of these funds. Outside education, the same foundations gave approximately $87 million (or 11 percent of their grants) to the humanities, up from $65 million (9 percent) in 1975. In the Foundation Center's category of humanities, the performing arts, museums, and music consistently received the most funds in the 1970s. Together they probably averaged at least 70 percent of grants for the humanities from 1975 to 1978. Dividing up the rest were the following, listed in descending order of amounts received: history, "general," art and architecture, language and literature, and philosophy (materials and computer analyses provided by the Foundation Center).

Foundations that give to the humanities vary markedly in size, mission, and geographic range. In general, the largest independent foundations (with assets of over $100 million) have staff and programs for education, if not specifically for the arts or humanities, and their giving tends to be regional or national in scope. These foundations give much more to higher education than to elementary and secondary education. A few fund research–fellowships (usually for faculty, not graduate students), interdisciplinary research, translations, new technologies for storing and distributing knowledge, and grants to learned societies, research libraries, institutes, journals, and university presses. Many large foundations fund curriculum and teaching: indirectly by means of institutional grants, often to private liberal arts colleges and occasionally to universities or community colleges; or directly through programs in general education, interdisciplinary and area studies, professional education, continuing education, and faculty development. The larger foundations also support major cultural institutions, projects that link the humanities to public affairs, and public broadcasting.

As a rule, many of the smaller independent foundations and community foundations do not have separate staff for education or the humanities. They concentrate on local health care and general service. What they give to education and culture tends to focus on local needs. These foundations usually do not support scholarship; they emphasize the importance of reaching nontraditional learners and people who have rarely used the community's cultural resources.

In spite of these differences, foundations of all sizes share a few characteristics. Grant categories often obscure projects that actually affect the humanities—for example, in general education, ethics, and cultural institutions. Foundations strongly prefer program grants to general operating support or discretionary grants, and they would rather seed a new project for a few years than sustain an ongoing program for a longer period. (There are, of course, exceptions to these rules. Some foundations give a good deal of discretion even in program grants; some also sustain programs and view novelty with skepticism.) Coordination of interests and resources among foundations is increasing (e.g., joint support of research libraries and the partnership between the Bush Foundation and the William and Flora Hewlett Foundation in support of traditionally Black four-year colleges), as it is between foundations, the NEH, and the State Humanities Committees affiliated with the NEH. Finally, foundations of all types want to encourage the application of knowledge to political, social, or ethical issues. Relatively few foundations support humanistic scholarship on a sustained basis; those that provide short-term support often stress the connection between scholarship and contemporary affairs.

Corporations

Corporate support for the humanities is more difficult to measure than that from foundations. Total corporate philanthropy in current dollars rose from $1.01 billion in 1968 to $2 billion in 1978. While this represents virtually no overall growth in constant (1968) dollars, corporate giving reversed a downward trend in the mid-1970s and increased about 18 percent in constant dollars from 1976 to 1978. According to the Conference Board (whose sample of reporting organizations includes corporations having foundations), about 36 percent of corporate contributions over the past few years has gone to education, with higher education receiving the lion's share (roughly 70 percent) of that.

Some of the support for higher education (approximately 30 percent in the Conference Board sample) takes the form of unrestricted operating grants and capital grants (including endowment) to institutions; ALCOA, for example, made unrestricted grants to sixty-six colleges and universities in 1978. How much of this funding helps the humanities is anyone's guess, but much of it goes to general education. Probably over 90 percent of contributions to specific fields goes to business, science, engineering, and public policy; of the much smaller amount going to humanistic fields, foreign languages and international studies apparently receive the most support.

A number of corporations have given substantially to the humanities. A few (including the General Electric Foundation and Exxon Education Foundation) have already contributed to the ACLS financial campaign, and some support research libraries and institutes; but most corporations have been reluctant to underwrite research in the humanities, especially the work of individual scholars. Corporate giving to the arts has increased dramatically over the past decade, most of it focused on highly visible activities. The percentage of their total contributions that corporations allocate for "culture and art" nearly doubled between 1968 (when the figure stood at about 5 percent) and 1978. Within this category in 1978, museums, music, and public broadcasting together received about 55 percent of the funds; arts funds or councils and cultural centers nearly 18 percent; theaters 6 percent; libraries (other than academic) 3 percent; dance 2 percent; most of the rest went to "other" and "not identifiable" subcategories. The Conference Board and most corporations do not mention the humanities as a subcategory (reports of the Conference Board, the Council for Financial Aid to Education, and the American Association of Fund-Raising Counsel).

The percentage of corporations that give has increased since the Filer Commission reported (1975) that only one-fifth of corporate taxpayers made charitable contributions, and that fewer than 10 percent of these contributors gave totals exceeding five hundred dollars. A growing number of corporations have programs for matching employee gifts, sometimes in a ratio as high as three to one. Many corporate contributions to the arts are claimed as business expenses rather than charitable deductions and are not included in the Conference Board's estimates of corporate philanthropy. Although these are encouraging signs of increasing support, a small percentage of businesses continues to account for a disproportionately large share of total corporate giving.

One frequently cited statistic has yet to improve significantly: corporate giving as a percentage of net income before taxes. The law allows corporations to deduct up to 5 percent of taxable income for charitable contributions. The Filer Commission recommended that all corporations contribute a minimum of 2 percent by 1980, but the figure remained at about 1 percent during the 1970s for all corporations and was even lower for larger corporations with pre-tax income over $25 million. A group of about thirty companies in Minneapolis-St. Paul has led the way in advocating and contributing the full 5 percent allowable. The members of this Minnesota Corporate Community 5 Percent Investment Club argue that corporations which fail to do so are, in effect, saying they think the government knows how to allocate these dollars more effectively than they can. *Corporate giving still has considerable capacity to expand.* Indeed this capacity is currently much greater than that possessed by independent foundations and represents the largest potential source of increased support from the private sector for valuable institutions and programs.

Some executives view the company-sponsored foundation as a means of expanding corporate philanthropy. (From 1975 to 1977, such foundations increased their giving by about 15 percent in constant 1968 dollars, while grants from independent foundations declined by about 1 percent in constant dollars.) In attitudes and priorities, corporate foundations fall somewhere between corporations and independent foundations. The corporate foundation does not have to answer directly to stockholders. It can build up reserves for use during lean business years, and it enjoys more flexibility in its funding policy—it can, for example, more easily give unrestricted grants. Company-sponsored foundations are more likely than corporations to base their giving on an explicit philanthropic mission, and more willing to support educational and cultural activities that might be classified as humanistic. They are less concerned with publicity than their parent companies and less inclined to justify support for culture in terms of the fringe benefits it will bring to employees. (The latter motive, on the other hand, benefits many communities, thanks to countless small corporations as well as the larger ones.) Still, the similarities between corporate foundations and their parents are greater than the differences. Applicants in the humanities should be aware of this, and realize that a long line of petitioners has already formed outside corporate doors, including many people who regard corporate philanthropy as the last, best, and limitless hope for support.

Some of the characteristics we have noted in independent foundations apply with equal or even greater force to corporations. Many corporations dislike discretionary or long-term sustaining grants. Few corporate foundations—and even fewer corporations—include the humanities in their conventional categories of funding; but there is room to comprehend and be more aware of the humanities under grants for general or liberal education, or for preprofessional or professional education. Indeed, corporations give quite generously to these areas of education and recognize the importance of communication, critical thinking, and values in a highly technological society. In general, corporations are reluctant to fund projects that may involve risks or criticism of social conditions, or to support cultural activity that does not have visible or immediate results. For these reasons, corporations tend to define culture narrowly as the arts, often failing to see the more subtle relationships between culture and the humanities. Corporations also have much less patience than do independent foundations for research not directed at specific economic, social, or technological problems.

The National Endowment for the Humanities

During the past fifteen years, the NEH has become the largest single benefactor for the humanities. Since its establishment in 1965, its mandate has been "to develop and encourage the pursuit of a national policy for the promotion of progress and scholarship in the humanities" (National Foundation on the Arts and the Humanities Act of 1965). As an advocate and a source of support, the Endowment has put the humanities on the map in the nation's capital, underscoring the conclusion of the Humanities Commission of 1964—that it is in the national interest for the federal government to give substantial support to the humanities. Being on the map in Washington has also sometimes politicized the humanities, to the dismay of humanists, politicians, and Endowment officials. Our aim in this section is not to give the reader an exhaustive account, but a generally affirmative glimpse of the NEH's diverse efforts to fulfill its mandate. To the extent that we offer criticism, it is sympathetic in spirit and constructive in purpose.

The Endowment's continual expansion in funding has been accompanied by change in the organization of its programs. From a modest beginning of $4.1 million in fiscal year (FY) 1967, definite funds for programs and planning have grown substantially to $100.3 million for FY1980 ($43.03 million in constant 1967 dollars as of January 1980). With additional appropriations of $12 million in matching funds, $27 million for Challenge Grants, and $10.8 million in administrative funds, total appropriations for 1980 amount to $150.1 million ($64.39 million in constant dollars). The 1976 reauthorization stipulated that at least 20 percent of the Endowment's program funds must be divided among the fifty State Humanities Committees, which then regrant the federal funds along with matching funds raised from various local sources.

A major theme in the expansion of the Endowment has been the encouragement of funding from private and state sources, by means of the gifts and matching and Challenge Grant mechanisms as well as through the specific terms of the legislation authorizing the state-based programs in 1976. Congress annually limits the sum that can be matched with federal money. The ceiling on matching funds has risen steadily, from $0.1 million in FY1967 to $12 million for FY1980. In most years since 1970, actual gifts to the agency have more than equaled the matching funds available. Increased private support for the humanities is also the goal of the Challenge Grant Program instituted in 1976 as part of the Endowment's reauthorizing legislation. Once a grant is approved, the recipient must match it three to one with funds from foundations, corporations, and other—mainly private—sources on which it has not drawn before, or with increased contributions from former donors. Unlike regular NEH program grants, which are made for particular projects of defined scope and duration, Challenge Grants may be used to cover ordinary operating costs, renovation of facilities, institutional development, and even the retirement of debt. Challenge Grant monies appropriated by Congress have grown quickly in current dollars from an initial level of $9 million in FY1977 to $27 million for FY1980.

The general goals and directions for the development of the Endowment's programs were determined in its first year. In the foreword to the *First Annual Report* (Washington, D.C., 1966), Chairman Barnaby Keeney wrote that "the overall challenge is to increase interest and use of the humanities by our citizens and to improve their access to them." The objectives outlined in the same report were the basis for the major program divisions which began making grants in FY1967: to aid scholars (Division of Fellowships); to develop and disseminate knowledge (Division of Research Grants); and to improve teaching of the humanities in schools and colleges and among the public (Divisions of Education and Public Programs). Since 1968 the NEH has given increasing priority to projects relating the humanities to important contemporary problems, values, and the general public. In 1979 the Endowment began to give special emphasis to American social history and the relationship between science, technology, and human values.

From the beginning, the *Division of Public Programs* has sought to stimulate public understanding and use of the humanities through "the development of the vehicles through which the humanities can be disseminated to the public—communications media, museums, historical organizations, and other such institutions"; and through "efforts to provide direct confrontation of the public with the humanities through regional activities, activities aimed at special segments of the public, and support for public conferences" (*Second Annual Report*, 1967).

In an effort to involve citizens with issues in "the humanities and public policy," the Division of Public Programs in 1971 sponsored experimental state-based programs in six states. By 1975 all fifty states had established separate activities, and in 1977 the affiliation of the state organizations with the NEH became the responsibility of the newly created *Division of State Programs*. The

State Committees (or Councils) are no longer required to focus their programs on the relation of the humanities to issues of public policy. Instead each state organization, through a broadly representative citizen's committee, acts as an independent funding agency, determining its own needs, programs, and guidelines.

The addition of matching funds (e.g., about $8 million in FY1979) significantly increases the actual amount of federal money for the *Division of Research Grants.* The division makes awards mostly in support of middle- or long-term projects, often involving collaboration among several professional humanists, in basic research, materials development and editing, and translations. In addition, it funds efforts to improve significant collections of research materials, supports scholarly conferences, and makes subventions for the publication of individual works. Recently the division has expressed a special interest in the writing of regional, state, and local histories.

The emphases of the *Division of Education Programs* have varied over the years, seemingly in step with the changing concerns of educators and the public. The spirit of civil rights reforms in the late 1960s was reflected in programs on the needs of culturally and educationally deprived Americans and on the contributions of minority cultures. In the early 1970s, the themes of urban and youth unrest informed projects that stressed the relevance of the humanities to contemporary social problems. The aftermath of the Watergate scandal brought a notable emphasis on ethics and values. In the Bicentennial year 1976, many projects capitalized on the resurgence of interest in American history. Until 1978 the division's program guidelines seem to have stressed interdisciplinary curricula and the improvement of instruction in the disciplines of the humanities. In 1978–79 the NEH gave special emphasis to foreign language study, continuing education, and the improvement of expository writing. Strengthening the humanities in graduate education for the professions has been a recurrent theme of the division's programs. Most of the division's funds support the development of curricula at colleges and universities. Grants in elementary and secondary education have fostered cooperation between schools and institutions of higher learning.

Through a variety of grant programs, from full- and half-year fellowships to stipends for summer study and participation in seminars, the *Division of Fellowships* supports advanced study. It does not fund research toward graduate degrees. The division supports individual study only (long-term and collaborative research projects are funded by the Division of Research Grants). In addition, the division has sponsored fellowships and seminars for the professions, funded individual fellowships awarded by research libraries, museums, and centers for advanced study, and provided assistance to the American Council of Learned Societies. Partly in response to criticism from educators and members of Congress that the agency has favored scholars from elite institutions, the Endowment has reorganized its fellowship programs so as to provide greater opportunities for humanists from two-year and smaller four-year institutions, as well as for young scholars from the larger and more prestigious universities.

Created in FY1979 to coordinate several grant programs not fitting easily into the five major program categories, the *Division of Special Programs* houses the NEH's Challenge Grant Program. It also administers the following: Program Development, an experimental arm of the Endowment that funds new approaches to programming for groups not traditionally associated with the humanities, such as labor unions, ethnic groups, and national adult membership organizations; Youthgrants in the Humanities, established in 1972 to give persons aged thirteen to thirty an opportunity to undertake projects in the humanities; NEH Youth Projects, a more recently created program seeking to reach young people through educational projects developed by national youth groups, museums, libraries, and other institutions; the Jefferson Lectures, inaugurated in 1971 to help relate humanistic learning to public affairs; and Courses by Newspaper (described above in chapter four). Also in the division is the program in Science, Technology, and Human Values, started in 1973 to coordinate support for a number of interdisciplinary projects funded by the agency's major divisions. At the same time the NEH and the National Science Foundation announced their joint administration of such projects, an area that both agencies need to expand.

The NEH has always had an office of planning, analysis, and evaluation. The broad tasks of what is now called the *Office of Planning and Policy Assessment* (OPPA) have remained generally the same over the years: the exploration and planning of new programs, the analysis and evaluation of current programs, and the dissemination of information about successful programs. The OPPA is part of the chairman's staff, and efforts are being made to strengthen the office's evaluative and analytical functions. As members of the NEH staff admit, "evaluation" is easier said than done, and the procedures and goals of evaluation have not yet been clearly defined. In fact, evaluation occurs in each division as well as in OPPA, which oversees evaluation. The NEH contracts for outside evaluations, conducts in-house evaluations, and requires many funded projects to evaluate themselves. The subjects examined include the external and particular (how effective is a specific project that NEH has funded?); the internal and budgetary (should changes be made in the percentage of the budget allocated to any division or program?); and the national and cultural (what is in the national interest?).

The portion of definite funds allocated to each of the Endowment's program divisions has varied over the years, reflecting organizational changes and changing emphases in the agency's mission. The earliest emphasis was on research and scholarship, with over 60 percent of program funds going to the Divisions of Fellowships and Research Grants in 1967 and 1968. The balance shifted in the years 1969–72, when the Division of Education Programs spent up to 44 percent of NEH program dollars. Since 1974 greater emphasis has been placed on public programs in the humanities, with increased allocations to the agency's Divisions of Public and State Programs. These changes are reflected in the graph on page 168.

Simply comparing the budgets of major program divisions does not give the full picture of the Endowment's priorities. Since 1978 the Endowment has emphasized four major goals:

To promote public understanding of the humanities, and of their value in thinking about the current conditions of national life; to

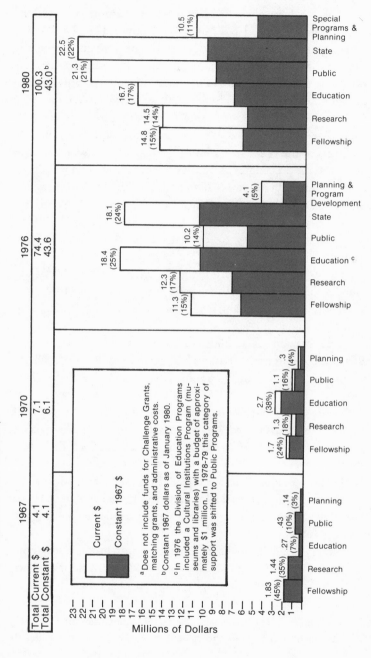

Definite Funds for NEH Program Divisions and Planning From FY 1967 to FY 1980 (in current and constant 1967 dollars[a])

improve the quality of teaching in the humanities and its responsive-
ness to new intellectual currents and changing social concerns; to
strengthen the scholarly foundation for humanistic study, and to
support research activity which enriches the life of the mind in
America; and to nurture the future well-being of those essential
institutional and human resources which make possible the study of
the humanities. ("Statement of the Chairman Before the Senate
Subcommittee on Education, Arts and the Humanities," June 1979)

Programs in pursuit of these goals cut across divisional lines.
For FY1980, the NEH estimates a distribution of nearly 55.4
percent of definite funds in the area of public understanding; that
represents the total of funds from Public Programs, State Programs,
Special Programs, and the fellowships for professions from the
Division of Fellowships. Teaching may receive 21.7 percent
(Education Programs, summer seminars from the Division of
Fellowships); scholarly research 22.2 percent (Fellowship Programs except those two just mentioned, Research Programs);
essential facilities 0.7 percent (Planning and Assessment Studies).
The portion for the last goal increases to 21.8 percent (and the
percentages for the other three goals drop to 43.6, 17.1, and 17.5
points, respectively) when funds appropriated for Challenge
Grants are added to definite funds, an indication of how heavily
the NEH depends on Challenge Grants for general support of
educational and cultural institutions.

Each of the Endowment's four goals is essential for the
vigorous life of the humanities, and the NEH's funds alone cannot
reach any of them. The nature of these broad goals and the
problems of funding have raised a number of issues related to the
Endowment, of which we consider these the most important:
coordination with other agencies; state programs in the humanities; the politics of the humanities; the relationship between federal
and private sources of support.

Other federal agencies support the humanities. Among these
the major ones are the National Endowment for the Arts (NEA),
Department of Education (including the National Institute of
Education, Fund for the Improvement of Postsecondary Educa-
tion, and Institute of Museum Services), Smithsonian Institution
(National Museum Act), and National Science Foundation

(NSF). The existence of these agencies does not in any way make the NEH's role less critically important. The Endowment is the only federal agency whose primary concern is the substance, methods, and disciplines of the humanities. It is the only agency where formal and nonformal modes of education in the humanities meet. Small by federal standards of staff and budget, the NEH is and should remain a large, indispensable, and separate part of the several sources of support by which Congress has determined to sustain the nation's cultural life.

The issue of coordination between the Endowment and other agencies can be exaggerated. Congress wants some coordination, but becomes suspicious when there seems to be too much of it—a signal that the process of appropriations must be faulty and that some sort of amalgamation of departments is needed. At the other extreme, a department's search for coordination may confess its failure to close a gap in its own organization and policies. Between these extremes exist various mechanisms and real needs for interdepartmental understanding.

Legislation charges the Federal Council on the Arts and Humanities with promoting coordination between the two Endowments and between them and other federal agencies. The Council consists of the chairmen of the Endowments and twelve other senior government officials, and its chairman is designated by the president. In October 1977, President Carter named Joseph Duffey concurrently chairman of the NEH and chairman of the Federal Council, and the administration indicated that it expected the Council to take a more active part in coordinating government policy than had previously been the case. The Council has indeed achieved interdepartmental "memoranda of understanding" on subjects such as museums, arts education, and cultural activities abroad. The Council has cooperated with the president's domestic policy staff in the still uncompleted task of defining major issues of cultural policy. But the degree and effect of the Council's efforts are uncertain, as is its future. By and large, most interdepartmental coordination takes place informally, in day-to-day contacts among staff who want to avoid duplication of effort by their respective agencies.

Informal liaison between the two Endowments occurs regularly in such program areas as arts education, museums, and the media. Legislative language and officials of both Endowments distinguish between the NEH's responsibility for history and interpretation of the arts, and the NEA's purview over the creation, display, and performance of major art forms. These lines of jurisdiction are sometimes obscure. Still, there is some conceptual validity and administrative utility behind the interdepartmental adage that "if the label is bigger than the picture," the NEH has jurisdiction. One can find the same logic in the interdepartmental memorandum of understanding on museums (NEH, NEA, Institute of Museum Services, National Science Foundation, and Smithsonian Institution, 3 May 1979): the NEH is to "support interpretive projects in museums in which the resources of the humanities are specifically brought to bear; that is, in which the social, historical and cultural contexts of objects and artifacts are emphasized in the presentation." In the program on Science, Technology, and Human Values, the NEH administers applications "in which the disciplines of the humanities will be prominently employed," while the NSF (Office of Science and Society— Ethics and Values in Science and Technology Program) handles proposals where the sciences are predominant or the balance between the humanities and sciences is unclear.

In spite of such arrangements, interdepartmental coordination remains inconsistent and tentative, partly because of the rigidity of lines drawn. This is especially true with respect to museums. Assigning certain kinds of project support to the NEH, NEA ("projects primarily in the arts"), and NSF ("projects primarily scientific or technical in nature") can reinforce distinctions between fields of knowledge even when these agencies—or particular museums—may want to encourage integration among them. Designating the budget of the Institute of Museum Services for general operating support tends to magnify the separation made by federal and private sources between programs and general expenses, when there is a need for a broad view of operating expenses and of the public and private responsibility to help fund them.

Coordination between the NEH and the former Office of Education (OE) was notably weak in elementary and secondary education, partly because of the size of OE and the complexity of the system of public education. We think the NEH has been deterred by its own internal priorities as well. In chapter two, we urged the NEH to strengthen its programs for schoolchildren and coordinate with the new Department of Education in the dissemination of exemplary programs. *Here we reemphasize our view that the NEH can most effectively support the humanities if it remains an independent resource and is not incorporated in the Department of Education.*

Coordination is neither an exact political science nor an easy practice. No area of national policy proves this more conclusively than does support for the humanities. Like defining the humanities, coordinating their sources of support is a difficult and continuous process. We have no simple formula unless it be this: avoiding duplication of effort ought not be the sole objective of coordination. The end should lie in the discovery of common or opposing assumptions about education and culture; in the assessment of how federal policy affects those who need support; and in the bending of lines of jurisdiction where appropriate.

Another and more controversial issue concerns the State Humanities Committees. In 1976 Senator Claiborne Pell (Democrat, Rhode Island, and chairman of the Senate Subcommittee on Education, Arts and Humanities) successfully opposed the reappointment of Ronald Berman as chairman of the NEH. The hearings were acrimonious, and the episode remains probably the most traumatic one in the history of the NEH. Senator Pell's major argument was—and still is, in spite of compromise legislation in 1976—that the State Humanities Committees need to be more accountable and responsive to state governments, and more attuned to the interests of the people. In brief, he contends that state programs should be conducted by state agencies, in the manner of State Arts Councils, not by committees that owe some allegiance to Washington.

Whereas originally the various State Humanities Committees were entirely separate from state government, the reauthorization of 1976 provided for appointment of two members in each state by the governor, and, in the event that the state legislature virtually matches the total federal grant, the governor has the further power to appoint half the members of the committee. No state has approached this level of appropriation, but the pending reauthorization of 1980 may increase the leverage of governors and state legislatures and could indeed lead to the transformation of State Committees into state agencies. In our view, the spontaneity and relative freedom from bureaucratic obstruction demonstrated by many State Committees more than outweigh any possible advantages of integrating them with the political system of the state. The State Committees have become a critically important link between federal support and the diversified and informal complex of voluntary associations. Although the record of their achievement is inevitably uneven from state to state or one period to another, they have shown themselves able to make fruitful contact with many groups in our society which have not previously engaged in humanistic endeavors. We would argue that some unevenness is in fact the price of freedom.

The controversy over State Committees is but one aspect of the politics of the humanities. Politics are imbedded in the notion of "promoting public understanding," in the belief that supporting the humanities is in the national interest, in the existence of a federal agency, and in the appointment of chairmen of the NEH. The politics of the humanities are confused, and sometimes needlessly polarized, by oversimplification of two major questions: national policy for the humanities; and the implications of promoting public consciousness.

We referred above to the Endowment's mandate "to develop and encourage the pursuit of a national policy for the promotion of progress and scholarship in the humanities." The legislation also refers to developing a "national policy of support for the humanities." The Surveys and Investigations Staff of the Committee on Appropriations (U.S. House of Representatives) misread this mandate when asserting that the NEH should develop a national policy for the humanities ("Report on the National Foundation on the Arts and the Humanities," March 1979). The legislation does not intend the NEH to set national policy for a field that is remarkable for its diversity and individualism.

Endowment officials emphasize that they try "to discern rather than define" what is in the national interest. They rely on the views of applicants, peer review panels, external inquiries into the state of the humanities, and the National Council on the Humanities. The Endowment's chairman presides over the Council, which has twenty-six other members "appointed by the President, by and with the advice and consent of the Senate, from private life." The chairman awards grants on the advice of the Council, which considers the recommendations of review panels and Endowment staff, but he is free to act contrary to the Council's advice.

By and large, this process means the Endowment reflects rather than shapes academic and public consciousness of the humanities. But the NEH has from the beginning also influenced the methods and directions of that consciousness. Chairmen have emphasized the need for scholars to reach large publics. Program guidelines encourage applicants to focus on a particular approach or problem; in the mid-1970s, for example, many museums began to prefer traveling exhibits to permanent ones after the NEH stressed this method in its guidelines. It is not unusual for the chairman and his staff to decide on specific emphases or changes in programs; recent examples include American social history and the reorganization of fellowship programs. The staff sometimes advises applicants to cast their proposals in a particular way, especially applicants who have had little or no practice in grantsmanship; occasionally such advice attaches conditions that applicants have not the staff or money to meet. Such influences derive ultimately from the fact that officials at the Endowment frequently interpret the agency's mission. Of all the participants in the review process, Endowment staff are the only ones who regularly consider what may or may not be in the national interest.

Although we do not want the NEH or any other agency to determine national cultural policy, we expect the NEH, like any agency, to define the contours of its field within reason. It should do so with more guidance from the National Council than has normally been the case, as the chairman and Council have recently acknowledged. The Council's charge includes advising the chairman "with respect to policies." This enables the Council to play an important policy role. It should see that the agency does not go beyond the intent of the authorizing legislation. The Council can help the Endowment clarify how a federal agency can promote public understanding of a field defined by countless private affirmations. Clarification is all the more necessary because some proponents and critics of the Endowment tend to discuss the politics of the humanities in ideological terms. Indeed, if the NEH becomes an ideological football, the fault will not be entirely that of the NEH, but of its critics as well.

The Endowment seeks to increase public consciousness through its programs, Challenge Grants, and matching funds. The aim is twofold. The public and various benefactors should know the meaning of the humanities, what they do, where they live, and why supporting them is in the national interest. Humanists and institutions should increase public access to the humanities. The NEH has worked diligently to achieve these important objectives, as many of the programs mentioned in this report testify. But the Endowment takes some risks and sometimes errs when it emphasizes public consciousness. Some institutions and individuals cannot find diverse sources of support as easily as others, for their scholarly needs may not relate directly to public life. The Endowment's concern over increasing its visibility in Washington and throughout the land has led it, on occasion, to confuse publicity with public consciousness or to overlook the essentially private side of the humanities. The NEH may inadvertently steer public attention away from educational and cultural institutions when it tries to reach specific groups through programs outside institutional settings. Finally, the preoccupation with adult public consciousness has meant relative neglect for an issue of vital consequence to citizens of all ages: the quality of education in our elementary and secondary schools.

The NEH has enlightened cultural debate by showing relationships between the humanities, culture, and public life. The Endowment might edify the debate still more by arguing the intrinsic value of the humanities; they cannot always merge with public consciousness through discussion of contemporary issues.

The relationship between the NEH and private sources of support involves attitudes as well as statistics. The Humanities Commission of 1964 recommended that the humanities receive a "plurality of support" from a wide range of sources, and this principle has been upheld by Congress, the Endowment, and private donors. In practice, however, the patterns and implications of plurality are not altogether reassuring.

In the 1950s and 1960s foundations often counted on the federal government to sustain successful projects that foundations had seeded. Foundations still prefer to fund experimental and innovative projects, but this same preference is evident in much of the funding provided by the NEH over the past fifteen years. We would argue that the NEH should not simply accept the traditional emphasis of many private sources on new projects as against support of operating expenses or long-term projects. Sustaining projects and institutions over the long term requires more federal responsibility than Congress or the NEH has undertaken so far.

Pressure on the NEH grows every year as the agency receives more and more applications. The agency relies increasingly on Challenge Grants and gifts and matching to meet the needs of applicants. Through Challenge Grants, the NEH and private sources do help sustain institutions. In two years, 1977 and 1978, donors contributed a total of $100.3 million ($51.4 million in constant 1967 dollars) through the Challenge Grant Program. The major share of this figure included $29.1 million from individuals; $38.5 million from foundations; $10.3 million from corporations and businesses; and $4.7 million from nonfederal governments. Of the $100.3 million, museums and historical organizations received $39.6 million; institutions of higher education $30.6 million; public libraries $2.3 million; research libraries $10 million; centers of advanced study $3.3 million; media organizations $7.3 million; national and local organizations $7.1 million; and other applicants $0.1 million.

Unquestionably, the Challenge Grant Program has been successful in helping institutions expand their financial bases and their public outreach. But Challenge Grants are not meant to provide ongoing federal support for operations: the grants are not renewable, and the number of grants represents only a fraction of the institutions eligible to apply. Apparently, one reason many institutions do not apply is their fear that they lack sufficient staff or public appeal for raising three matching dollars for every federal dollar. The same anxiety is evident in institutions advised to seek outside gifts to match federal dollars in support of specific programs; universities, museums, research libraries and centers, and university presses have particular difficulty raising private funds for activities that seem of special benefit to individual scholars. In short, the problems of sustaining programs or preserving cultural institutions have been addressed but are very far from being solved by Challenge Grants or gifts and matching. Their solution requires that federal agencies and private sources assume a general responsibility for supporting the operating expenses of cultural institutions.

Whether these problems can be solved will also depend on the answers to two questions. How much can nonfederal support of the humanities expand? How resilient will applicants be when required to search widely and continuously for funding? Although we cannot define them exactly, we think there are limits in both cases. Federal ceilings on Challenge Grants and matching funds should be raised in increments that are not too far ahead of estimated increases in nonfederal funding. If corporations increase their contributions as they have the capacity to do, private funding can grow considerably. Applicants should not be required to overburden their staff, distort their primary mission, or come up with something new in order to obtain matching funds; the Challenge Grant Program affects institutions as well as sources of funds. Most important, the federal government should relax its restrictions on the use of tax dollars to preserve cultural institutions. The policy needs to be revised that limits any institutional applicant to one Challenge Grant; in many cases, reducing the three-to-one ratio can make a real difference to the institution's success. The NEH and other agencies should have more discretion to sustain institutions over the long term; the NEH should redouble its recent efforts in this direction.

Any change in federal funding of the humanities will affect the policies of private sources. Some foundations and corporations see federal matching programs as undermining the autonomy of their own funding programs. In the main, however, private sources welcome evidence of government support; they can then choose how to supplement that support, avoid duplicating it, or simply draw from it the encouragement to maintain their funding of the humanities. In the past few years, the Challenge Grant Program has caused federal and private officials to increase the collaboration that had already been stimulated by other joint ventures in support of the humanities.

In spite of the difficulties outlined above, the Endowment's record is commendable. The staff is conscientious and responsive to critical suggestions from outside. Except for elementary and secondary education, the NEH has made steady progress in implementing its mandate. The ideal of connecting scholarly knowledge and public consciousness is elusive, and the truth that support for the humanities is in the national interest will never be self-evident to millions of citizens. A federal agency dedicated to this ideal and truth is profoundly important to cultural life in the United States.

The following recommendations are not exhaustive. They indicate where sources should concentrate support for the next decade. The highest priorities for increased funding are elementary and secondary education, research, and the operating expenses of cultural institutions. Funds should also go toward improving post-secondary curricula and interpretive programs beyond educational institutions. Sources can support these areas in ways consistent with their respective interests and geographic scope. This point has to be emphasized with respect to advanced training or research, whose importance has been insufficiently recognized by many agencies of support, private and public. Research in any field helps keep it alive intellectually, and this vitality infuses formal and informal learning. Maintaining the system of research—notably fellowships, libraries, and institutes—should not be left entirely to the federal government. It is also the responsibility of governing boards of colleges and universities, foundations, and corporations. We turn first to corporations because we would emphasize the unfulfilled potential of corporate support for the humanities.

RECOMMENDATION 29:   Corporations should follow the lead of the Minnesota Corporate Community 5 Percent Investment Club and more fully use the allowable 5 percent of their pre-tax income that may be deducted for charitable contributions. The national average is only 1 percent, leaving a 4 percent margin still available. Corporations should increase the percentage of contributions to the humanities. More specifically, they should concentrate on the following: development of critical skills in elementary and secondary education; programs of collaboration between schools and local cultural institutions; programs that relate the humanities to vocational, professional, and scientific education; broad programs of research; collaboration between educational and cultural institutions in programs of continuing education for vocational and professional audiences; operating expenses of museums and libraries; local media programs with an emphasis on the humanities and public affairs. The American Association for the Advancement of the Humanities should prepare a guide to the possible forms of collaboration between businesses and humanists, and should explore means for maintaining permanent links between them.

RECOMMENDATION 30:   Foundations should increase their support of the following neglected areas: professional development for schoolteachers; programs of collaboration between schools and colleges; professional development for faculty at two-year colleges; fellowships for humanists and funds for basic research; collaboration between research libraries and regional educational and cultural institutions; operating expenses and interpretive programs in local museums and historical societies.

RECOMMENDATION 31:   Federal agencies (including the NEH) should increase their general support for cultural preservation in museums, libraries, and historical societies. Federal agencies should encourage the development of programs in elementary and secondary education that recognize critical thinking as a basic skill, programs that include the humanities in basic education for adults, and interdisciplinary programs in the humanities, science, and technology. Congress should fund a limited number of graduate fellowships, advance the program budget of the NEH at least to keep pace with inflation, and gradually raise the ceilings on Challenge Grants and matching funds as conditions allow. The NEH should increase its percentage of funding for elementary and secondary education, public programs on the humanities in elementary and secondary education, and research.

INDEX 🌿